Debra's Healing Kitchen
CONNECTING MIND, BODY & SPIRIT

A Simplified Guide to
Healthy Living
Vegetarian & Vegan Recipes and More

A SIMPLIFIED GUIDE TO HEALTHY LIVING: VEGETARIAN & VEGAN RECIPES AND MORE

1405 SW 6th Avenue • Ocala, Florida 34471 • Phone 800-814-1132 • Fax 352-622-1875
Website: www.atlantic-pub.com • Email: sales@atlantic-pub.com
SAN Number: 268-1250

Library of Congress Cataloging-in-Publication Data

Names: Peek-Haynes, Debra, author.
Title: A simplified guide to healthy living : vegetarian & vegan recipes and more / by Debra Peek-Haynes.
Description: Ocala, Florida : Atlantic Publishing Group, INC., [2018] | Includes bibliographical references and index.
Identifiers: LCCN 2018008427 (print) | LCCN 2018018782 (ebook) | ISBN 9781620235898 (ebook) |
    ISBN 9781620235881 (pbk. : alk. paper) | ISBN 1620235889 (alk. paper)
Subjects: LCSH: Cooking (Natural foods) | Health. | LCGFT: Cookbooks.
Classification: LCC TX741 (ebook) | LCC TX741 .P43 2018 (print) | DDC 641.5/636—dc23
LC record available at https://lccn.loc.gov/2018008427

Printed in the United States

PROJECT MANAGER: Danielle Lieneman
INTERIOR LAYOUT AND JACKET DESIGN: Sederrick Raphiel

Acknowledgments

I want to thank my Lord and Savior, Jesus Christ for giving me the ability, strength, experience, and opportunity to write this book. Without Him, I could do nothing.

I want to acknowledge my husband, Dr. Frederick D. Haynes, III, for being my most consistent and patient guinea pig. He has never demanded that I cook but has accepted whatever I have prepared. He has been with me through my evolution from being a down home soul food cook to becoming a down home health soul food cook. He ate my macrobiotic cooking and everything else in between when we were trying to conceive our child (*see my story on my website*).

I also want to thank my precious gem, our daughter, Abeni Jewel. I am blessed abundantly that she enjoys eating my cooking. Abeni is sweet, kind, and very bright. Through God's blessing, lots of prayers, and healthy eating, we had a special delivery from the angels.

Last but not least, I want to acknowledge the loving memory of my parents, Elizabeth and Vassie Peek. I was blessed with their unconditional love, wisdom, affection, and encouragement. They never ceased to let me know I could do great things. They taught me the necessity to be generous towards other people and to always be grateful. Thank you to my loving siblings, Lonnie and Patty, all of my family and special dear friends who love me and support all that I do. I am forever grateful for all of you!

Special thank you to **Soror Thalia Matherson** for your assistance and **Phyllis Hill** for helping me complete my first book.

Dedication

Dear godmother, Rachel Simms James, thank you for your
unconditional love. You bridged the gap when my mother,
your dear friend, went to be with the Lord.
Now you have joined "The Great Cloud of Witnesses."
You left a legacy of love and memories of good food!

CONTENTS

Part 1: Understanding Healthy Eating

Part 2: Recipes

Part 3: Cooking for Children

Introduction

MY PURPOSE FOR WRITING THIS BOOK

For the past 10 or more years, I have been asked to write a cookbook. For the life of me, I cannot figure out why I have been opposed to this request, other than to say I had not made up my mind to commit the time and mental energy to such a worthy project. However, I must admit I wondered at times if I knew enough or had enough of the right information to share.

Whenever, I make presentations regarding my healthy lectures, I am amazed at how much information I have gathered. Sometimes when a talent or interest is second nature, you tend to take it for granted. The past 25 years have been a tremendous learning experience in my walk to better my health and the health of all those whose lives are connected to mine.

MEMORIES

There are so many wonderful cookbooks that offer healthy information and delicious recipes. My goal is to present something that is not intimidating to people who really want to make a change in their health and who also enjoy eating. I am a real foodie. I love to eat good quality food. I think about food all of the time and enjoy it when others delight in what I prepare. Of all the foods in the world, I enjoy soul food the best. First, it reminds me of growing up on the shores of New Jersey with my family. Although my brother, sister, and I were born in New Jersey, we were blessed with strong southern roots from our parents. Both of our parents could cook. We had balanced meals that were always prepared with love.

Love is an element that is often missing in our meal preparation. Secondly, food should taste and look good. Soul food by its mere name can accomplish both goals. Thirdly, I believe soul food is food that should provide comfort and eating pleasure. Look up the history of soul food as it relates to slavery to understand why. I hope this book can inspire someone who hates cooking to find the love element in the process. It would be a great study to track children who were raised in families that had loving parents, guardians, and caretakers who were able to prepare healthy meals, as opposed to children raised in homes without home-prepared meals. It would be interesting to see how the children were affected. Meals don't have to necessarily be prepared by the parents in the home, but by the right person with the right attitude to help create a healthy environment.

IS THERE LOVE IN THE FOOD?

In preparation for this book, I spoke with my holistic doctor, Dr. Jewel Pookrum, about the importance of food being prepared with love. That immediately reminded me that my parents often prepared holiday meals together. It was a wonderful experience living with loving parents that could both cook!

I do not recall my mother ever coming to the kitchen to cook without being fully dressed. I was raised in a time when women in my community took pride in their appearance when preparing food and throughout their daily responsibilities.

Here are some suggestions given to me by Dr. Pookrum regarding food preparation:
1. Make sure you are not bitter or have ill intent during meal planning and preparation.
2. Say a prayer before you begin cooking.
3. Have a purposeful intent for the meal. Who needs healing?
   Focus on how you want your loved ones to feel and benefit from the meal.
4. Breath with focus.
5. Our physical appearance and our demeanor is important, so make it a priority.
6. Taste and appearance should comfort and stimulate the eating pleasure.
7. Remember healing life can come from the right foods and attitude.

It has been my pleasure to provide healthy and tasty food to my family and loved ones. My husband and daughter have been my constant guinea pigs. Sometimes, I am so on it with my recipes, while other times they politely point out that something went wrong. Please don't be hard on yourself when you prepare the forthcoming recipes. You may want to adjust some of the seasoning. Always leave room to try again.

ONE MORE THING

Many of you have cooks in your family who never measure ingredients. They somehow intuitively know just how much of this or that to add to their dishes. I am one of those cooks, but recently I have worked on writing down measurements and ingredients. Some recipes have come about because of a certain mood or memory that I wanted to create. I am not presenting a foolproof cookbook, but one that provides a basis for healthy, enjoyable eating.

OVERCOMING PERSONAL HEALTH CHALLENGES

My mother always checked with me to make sure I eliminated every day. At the time, I was a bit bothered by her daily inquiry. However, now I have an appreciation and understanding about her care for me.

She believed in having a "good cleaning out" as she would say, which means elimination. I always remember feeling a little lighter after a mild cleansing. After meeting my holistic doctor, I learned more about my digestive system and why I probably had issues much of my earlier life. Eating more fiber, drinking more water, massages (this helps the nervous system),exercising*, and taking probiotics** have greatly helped my digestion. However, with challenges of not enough rest, it has become necessary for me to pay closer attention to my digestive system. Therefore, on her advice, I have increased probiotics. I learned through my experience, consultations, and research that the body ages because of toxins.

We are overwhelmed with toxins from medication, the environment, toxic cleaning products, and anything that alters our bodies and minds from the ability to navigate and overcome daily and life challenges. Therefore, it is necessary to make adjustments in our daily food consumption to offset these challenges. A Rule of Thumb from many holistic health professionals, if you have a serious illness, eat foods that grow within 300 miles of where you reside. These foods are more in tune to your body and what it needs.

Exercise does not have to be complicated to be effective. Constant movement for 30 minutes (15 minutes in each interval) total each day will help keep your body including your internal organs toned. Using your body weight for planks and push ups can further help keep your core (stomach and back muscles) and arms toned.

**Probiotics not only include supplements that come in pill form, but also consuming fermented foods. We all carry good bacteria in our gut (digestive system) that help to breakdown and absorb nutrients. If you have health conditions, it is likely you are deficient of adequate good bacteria strains. Among other symptoms, this can cause bloating, constipation, and nutrient deficiencies. To alleviate these issues, include fermented (pickled) food in your diet, including pickled cucumbers, beets, kimchi, sauerkraut, and miso paste. If you need to limit your sodium intake, you can adjust the miso paste servings for your soups and marinades.*

Basic Tips for Beginning a Healthier Lifestyle

1. What is your purpose? Decide what is important enough to make you want a better quality of life.

2. Be careful how much time you spend with people that are negative and do not have your best interest at heart. Spend some time with people that love and celebrate you. Make sure you share love too.

3. Don't ignore long-term depression. Seek counseling and don't stop until you find the right counselor for you! It may take more than one try but you must get help. Also, check your diet. Certain foods are beneficial for better emotional health.

4. Take an assessment of your living environment. It doesn't matter if you live in a modest apartment or house. Keep it clean and organized. This will help your mood and lessen stress.

5. How much organic produce do you have in your refrigerator on a weekly basis? Do you have a variety of fruits and vegetables? I am not including corn and potatoes. You need dark green leafy vegetables and produce with many colors.

6. Invest in books that provide information on healthy lifestyles, mental health, foods, and exercise.

7. Find a good internist (holistic is best), chiropractor, and massage therapist.

8. Remember to spend some time in the sun for natural vitamin D3, dependent on how much melanin your skin contains.

9. Throw away white sugar, white flour, and processed foods. Foods should be as minimally processed as possible. See my list of substitutions for sweeteners.

10. Make sure you eliminate daily and take an herbal cleanser after periods of stress, sickness, or travel to help your body cleanse itself of toxins that can cause disease.

11. Love yourself so you can better love others. How do you think about you? How do you treat you?

12. Meditate and pray. Find a time of silence each day to keep your body centered and your mind sharp. Too much noise can interrupt what God might be trying to tell you.

13. Make sure you prioritize restful sleep. Don't discount the importance of getting enough rest. There is no substitution.

14. Don't get dismayed when you fall off the health wagon. Dust yourself off and start again.

15. Seek to maintain a healthy weight. Remember you want to be healthy, not just thin. Thin people can also be unhealthy, depending on their dietary and living habits.

16. Make sure you drink quality water and not straight from the tap. Invest in a filter for home if at all possible. Drink good spring water in bottles made without harmful toxins.

17. Your health is your responsibility, so seek information for yourself from more than one source. Weigh what you learned and make a good decision for yourself. Being uninformed about your body is not healthy! What is your financial, emotional and physical commitment to yourself?

PART 1

Understanding Healthy Eating

CHAPTER 1

Getting Started

One of the most important things to have in any situation is a willing spirit and open mind. This is most important when you attempt to prepare a healthy meal, quick or involved.

Many recipes I loved as a child, I have tweaked the ingredients to make a more healthy food preparation. If you have recipes you love, keep them and see if using healthy but similar ingredients provide you with a taste that is not only similar, but healthier. It is my opinion that this does not work for recipes with pork, beef, or heavy cream. I prefer to avoid these items because there are so many other foods we can eat. Pork, beef, and dairy cream can carry so many health risks. They are not necessary unless you only have those items available to you. For most of us, this is not the case. I suggest avoiding these foods if at all possible.

CHAPTER 2

Key Ingredients and Healthier Substitutions

INSTEAD of plain tap water to wash fruits and vegetables, USE a Quality Veggie Fruit and Vegetable Wash or Alkaline Water. There have been many controversies regarding toxic chemicals found in tap water, so please use filtered water when possible.

INSTEAD of dairy milk, USE plant-Based such as almond, oat, coconut, or hemp (some of these milks are richer in taste than others). Make sure you use the ones that have the desired consistency for your dish. Please be careful with all soy products because of the GMO issue. Make sure you use only organic soy products when available.

INSTEAD of butter, USE Earth Balance™ Buttery Spread (this product provides a great taste without the hydrogenated oils that can clog the arteries; available in a tub or sticks for baking). There are coconut-based products as well. I much prefer coconut oil-based butter substitutes. Some health professionals suggest using clarified butter, called Gee, because of the healthy fatty acids that can be helpful for chronic infections. Gee is the clear substance that has all of the unhealthy substances removed.

INSTEAD of vegetable Oil, USE safflower, olive, coconut, sesame, walnut, avocado, Macadamia nut (there are other oils like apricot oil that I use in baking, which works well and has better health benefits than regular vegetable oil). Please stay away from corn oil, regular vegetable oil, canola oil, and regular shortening. Choose oils that are high in polyunsaturated and monounsaturated fats. Poly tends to lower cholesterol levels and mono tends to lower LDL (lower-density lipoprotein), bad cholesterol levels.

Make sure you check the bottle to see which oils are recommended for low, medium, or high heat. Many would suggest olive oil only be used in low heat or room temperature.

INSTEAD of table salt, USE sea salt. Sea salt has minerals intact so it is not pure sodium; regular table salt is almost pure sodium. Sea salt tends to have a more pungent taste, so you don't need to use as much for seasoning. There has been some controversy regarding sea alt versus table salt. In my personal studies, I am comfortable with using sea salt, especially Himalayan, whenever available. Sea salt has naturally occurring minerals that we must have for proper bodily function. Other varieties that can be beneficial are Celtic Sea Salt and French Grey Sea Salt.

INSTEAD of seasoning salt, USE Herbamare™. This seasoning contains sea salt and a variety of high quality herbs. Make sure you don't use any seasoning that contains monosodium glutamate or MSG. This is a dangerous ingredient that can cause damage to your nervous system and it is high in sodium. This often causes headaches and other side effects. When dining out, make sure you ask the restaurant if they use this ingredient.

Instead of white sugar (white sugar has been listed in many studies about its negative affects on emotions and additions), Use raw turbinado, unbleached cane sugar, agave, Stevia, or maple syrup. Maple syrup has a lower glycemic index than other sweeteners but it also contains beneficial nutrients. Some diabetics can also try coconut sugar because of its low glycemic index. It also has some nutritional benefits. Its consistency is similar to raw sugar granules, so it can be used for baking. I have had good reports from people that used it for their baked recipes. Avoid white sugar because it is bleached and highly processed and striped of its nutrients. Turbinado sugar has minerals intact, so it dissolves slower in the system.

INSTEAD of white rice, USE organic wild rice or brown rice, which have fiber and minerals intact. White rice breaks down into sugar within the body's system much quicker than brown. Brown rice and wild rice are complex carbohydrates that provide much higher fiber benefits than white rice.

INSTEAD of white flour, use whole-wheat pastry flour, unbleached barley, spelt flour, almond, and oat flours. White flour has less fiber than whole-wheat or other whole-grain flours. Eating a diet heavy in white flour products causes constipation and can be very toxic. Diabetics need to switch to whole-grain flour products because of the nutrients and fiber; complex carbohydrates are much better for our digestive system. Almond flour has been used for people that have gluten allergies. It provides a texture similar to whole-wheat Flour.

INSTEAD of regular apple cider vinegar, USE unfiltered organic apple cider vinegar. This is an ingredient that has multiple uses. It can be medicinal and also provide fabulous flavor to many dishes. For example, organic apple cider vinegar is a key ingredient in my coleslaw and potato salad.

INSTEAD of corn starch, USE Kudzu root starch. This product comes from the genus Pueraria in the pea family Fabaceae, subfamily Faboideae. It is a climbing, coiling, and trailing vine native to southern Japan and southeast China and is used in many Asian dishes. Use this in recipes that need thickening. This product is recommended because it is a great aid for digestion and can be purchased at most health food stores. Corn starch is widely used in many food products but is high in sugar and many times products will contain sugar and corn syrup, which is not a good combination. Make sure you avoid eating these types of products because it can have an adverse affect on your health, especially if you are fighting diabetes.

Try your best to buy organic products. You want to limit all pesticides from your diet and any genetically produced produce such as corn and soybeans. In years to come, we will fully realize the havoc that these genetically engineered foods have had on our health.

CHAPTER 3

The Importance of Knowing Your Water

In recent years and months, we have heard so much news about water. The Flint crisis has made headlines and has caused a heightened awareness of our decaying infrastructure. We must not take this situation lightly because more and more we will hear about the lack of access to clean water in communities in the United States. Unfortunately, this crisis has affected high percentages of African-Americans, Hispanics, and people below the poverty level. The water issue has been at crisis level for many years in other countries around the world. Some of us have not been informed or have taken the posture that this could not happen to us. We must become more aware and be informed. The more information at our disposal means the more power we have to make better choices for family, our communities, and ourselves.

Our municipal water systems contain many toxic substances. Even if you have copper pipes installed in your home, the water is still traveling from the municipal pipes that are mostly lead-based. According to health professionals, the water filtration system does not remove drugs that have been secreted through human elimination. As has been highlighted in many news reports, the United States population is highly addicted to drugs and unnatural healing treatments. Therefore, our water has been contaminated with diabetic, high blood pressure, and many other types of medication. For good health, we must use home filtration for our drinking water. Here are some suggested filters to consider:

1. Sears Home Filtration Products
2. Brita Pitcher Filters
3. Pure Filters
4. Alkaline Water Systems

Water is an essential element necessary for good health. Most of us are dehydrated or we do not drink high quality water. Plastic is not always the best container for water, so it is important to make sure the water is contained in plastics without BPA or other chemicals that can leak into the water. Many bottling companies now have information on the bottles regarding being BPA free. If available, glass bottles are a good material to contain water. Spring water bottled at the source is a good choice for most people. Read the label to see the location where the water was sourced There are conditions where spring water is not the best choice.

If you have serious physical conditions, please make sure you consult with your healthcare professional. In addition, make sure you do your research. It is always better if you are informed so you understand your options. There are many books on the subject, but for a good beginning I suggest reading *Water: The Ultimate Cure* by Steve Meyerowitz. ***There is a fascinating and powerful study about how to activate healing benefits of water by Dr. Emoto Masaru water experiment. Please Google.***

CHAPTER 4

Suggestions to Add to Your Grocery List

Have an open mind when you switch to these suggested ingredients. None of these suggestions will work if you are closed-minded and unwilling to make changes.

FOR BEGINNERS

If you have recipes that you can't live without, use the suggested natural options on the list to assist with making your change. Don't get discouraged if a recipe doesn't turn out the way you planned; it might take several tries before you get the right consistency with your recipes. Instead of using whole eggs for recipes, try using egg whites only; you may have to use two egg whites in the place of one whole egg.

Remember to make changes on a consistent basis. If you have a life-threatening illness or chronic aliment, it is most important for you to make immediate changes if you are striving to live a healthier life.

A BEGINNERS GROCERY LIST

Many of you may find a few products that are unfamiliar listed in my "Instead of List." These items were so helpful to me that I wanted to share them with you. For example, my digestive system has greatly benefited from the Kombu Seaweed. My hair is now healthier and looks great when I'm consistently consuming this plant.

Kombu or Wakami Sea Vegetables: Both of these plants are from the seaweed family and are known to be very beneficial, especially because of their iodine content. Iodine is an essential mineral that is necessary for proper thyroid function. The lack of iodine has been associated with the susceptibility to cancer and other illnesses. It assists with digestion, providing lots of trace minerals, and can even aid in strengthening the hair. It also provides a mild salty taste. I often use an inch of soaked Kombu to cook in my beans to avoid the gas affect. This plant can also be used to make supplemental baby organic brown rice milk. Additionally, Wakami is another good supplement to miso and other healing soups. One regular bag of seaweed can last for months. You can find these products at most health food and Asian grocery stores.

The following list is full of "must haves" for your kitchen. Purchase these items from your local health food store and add them to your pantry for healthier recipes. If any of these items are not in stock, ask the store manager to order them for you:

- Coconut sugar
- Raw apple cider vinegar (available at most grocery stores)
- Raw turbinado sugar
- Kudzu root starch (used for sauces and helps digestion)
- Organic brown rice (short grain for fall and winter and long grain for spring and summer)
- Whole-grain or unbleached flour
- Sea salt (fine grain)
- Raw coconut oil (good for sauté recipes and can be used in baking)
- Safflower oil (good for high temperatures and a favorite for my greens)
- Avocado oil (this has become a new favorite. It works well with my greens recipe)
- Earth Balance™ Buttery Spread (it's non-hydrogenated)
- Nutiva coconut Buttery Spread (I like this product because it's non-hydrogenated, does not include canola oil, and has a buttery taste)
- Irish moss (contains trace minerals and vitamin B9 taken from the Atlantic Ocean)
- Kombu sea vegetable (use this when preparing your beans. It provides minerals as it reduces bloating and gas because of its ability to aid in digesting beans)

CHAPTER 5

Food for Thought Regarding Your State of Health

Please keep in mind that food has a huge impact on our survival, vitality, and overall well-being. With this in mind, if you have a potentially fatal illness, it is most important that you not only change your eating habits rapidly but also examine your emotional state. Your body needs proper fuel for better health, but do not neglect the importance of your mind. Suppressing trauma, loss, or other issues can negatively impact our health. We must not suppress what happens to us, but we must find the right therapist to assist us in emotional healing. We must not live in the past but learn and bring wisdom from what we have come through and move forward.

There are so many resources for natural healing, but we must have an open mind. As I always remind myself and others that have health issues, "God does not operate in a box." Surely, he gave us provisions for healing. Our doctors are supposed to be our partners in our healing, not our gods. Seek good advice, do your own research, pray, meditate, and then make the best decision for you.

If you have heart disease, consider eliminating fried food from your diet and confront issues that have given you a sad or broken heart. You cannot continue eating processed foods with lots of hidden fat, sodium, and sugar. You must increase fiber by eating whole grains, beans, and fresh produce.

By reading this book, you are embarking upon a journey of opening your mind to feeling better and being healthier.

CHAPTER 6
Eating on a Budget

Please know that budget does not mean LACK. We must assess how we best use our resources more efficiently. Whenever, I feel my resources are limited, I have to check my thought process, review my actions, and remind myself that my heavenly father has all that I need. It is up to me to believe and act like it.

I have heard many comments about the high cost of eating healthy. My response is always, "You are either going to pay in the beginning or in the end." Meaning, if you choose not to give your body what it needs to be healthy, you will have to pay on the back end with lost time from work, larger health bills, and missed quality time with family and friends.

Eating fast food sometimes appears to be a convenience and costs less than eating foods prepared at home. However, a diet consistent of fast foods on a weekly, and especially daily, consumption will cause a huge inconvenience because of its health consequences. Being sick is much more expensive than eating high quality food. Some of the barriers many people face are access to fresh produce. Even those with access do not always know how to shop healthier. Most of the challenges regarding our health result from not spending time thinking about how to make better decisions. If we believed and understood the importance of what we do to our bodies, I believe we would start making better choices. In order to save money, you must have some home-prepared meals. This doesn't have to take a lot of time, just some thought. I hope some of my suggestions in this book will help you decide to change your approach if you haven't taken time to prepare home cooked meals. Eating home cooked meals, even if only a few times a week, can make a difference.

SUGGESTIONS FOR SEEKING PRODUCE:
1. Local farmers markets can offer good value for fresh produce.
2. Urban gardens are on the rise in many cities and towns throughout the country.
3. Consider growing vegetables in your back yard or wherever you can fit pots in the sun light
4. Buy in bulk and split the produce with a friend
5. Look for sales of organic produce in health food stores

Eating on a Budget (*continued*)

For example, if you have a family of four or more, you can eat on a low-cost budget by buying the following items (buy organic whenever possible):

- Organic Brown Rice: a whole-grain; try long grain to transition from white rice – buying in bulk is generally less expensive
- Millet: a whole grain that is inexpensive, but with lots of benefits
- Bunch of greens: turnip, mustard, and collards; best prices from a farmers or urban market
- Green beans
- Onions: keep these to season all types of foods and dishes
- Beans: buy kidney, white, navy, lentils, black beans – these are generally inexpensive and very healthy. Try purchasing them in bulk from health food stores in order to save money. These foods are high in fiber and they can also be used as a protein substitute.
- Carrots: compare buying bagged carrots to buying loose carrots
- Bagged apples are available all year-round compared to pears being at their peak only in the fall
- Bag of oranges: cost less when buying in bulk
- A loaf of whole-grain bread – you can increase the use by cutting slices in half
- Organic Tofu can be substituted for meat. Soybeans are being genetically altered, so it's important to read the label and make sure that it says it's not GMO or it's organic. Tempeh may be better for men. Seitan is a good substitute if you do not have any gluten allergies. There are other meat substitutes that contain protein from plants. Make sure you read the labels and know what is in your food. If it is genetically modified (GMO), please avoid.
- Always save the stalks of greens to use for making vegetable soup and bean stock. Keep the hard broccoli stalks and use them as well. Try and use the whole vegetable instead of discarding leaves and stalks that have a lot of nutrients.

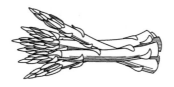

CHAPTER 7

Resources

WONDERFUL FOODS THAT HEAL

Deuteronomy 8:7-9 For the Lord your God is bringing you into a good land — a land with streams and pools of water, with springs flowing in the valleys and hills; a land with wheat and barley, vines and fig trees, pomegranates, olive oil and honey; a land where bread will not be scarce and you will lack nothing.

God's bounty is filling and more than sufficient. He has provided us with wonderful fruits, vegetables, grains, fish, and fowl to keep us healthy and satisfied. They taste good and are loaded with nutrients, vitamins and other healing properties. Please purchase organic produce as often as possible. Pesticides can damage your health.

PRODUCE	BENEFIT	VITAMINS & MINERALS
Apple	About half of the recommended daily allowance of vitamin C is right under the skin of the apple. The skin is also an excellent source of fiber. Apples should be firm and without bruising.	A great source of fiber, along with vitamin C.
Asparagus	In order to assist your body in absorbing Vitamins K and A, ("fat-soluble" nutrients) it's best to eat this vegetable with a little fat such as olive oil, which is a soluble nutrient.	Contains four cancer fighters: Vitamins A, C, K, and Folate.

PRODUCE	BENEFIT	VITAMINS & MINERALS
Berries	All berries should be stored unwashed until use and in their original containers. Some of the more popular berries are blueberries, blackberries, cranberries, currants, gooseberries, raspberries, and strawberries. All should be kept dry and refrigerated; cranberries are best when they have a soft hazy white coating or a bloom. All listed berries are very high in antioxidants. Avoid seedy tips and white shoulders on the currants, gooseberries, strawberries.	Berries that are plump, symmetrical, bright and rich in color are a good source of vitamin C. All possess antioxidant properties and are beneficial for the heart.
Broccoli	Can be eaten raw or cooked. When selecting broccoli, look for bunches that are vivid in color. The more bright green, purplish, or blue-green in color, the more beta-carotene and vitamin C that is present.	Rich in folate, fiber, magnesium, phosphorus, and potassium; broccoli also provides an excellent source of vitamins A, B6, C, E, and K.
Organic brown rice	Brown rice is the whole rice kernel with only the hull removed. Some studies have shown that eating brown rice may lower the incidence of cancer in the large intestine and the colon. Eating brown rice is also an excellent way to lower your high glycemic index, thus lowering your blood sugar levels.	Brown rice is high in fiber, vitamin B6, and niacin. The sweet and nutty texture is a wonderful source of manganese, magnesium, and selenium.
Carrots	Choose carrots that are smooth, firm, and brightly colored. Carrots that are more slender than thick tend to be sweeter. Their sugar content is second only to beets. The deeper the orange color, the higher the beta carotene content. Since the carrot is a tap root, remove the tops as quickly as possible in order to preserve the vitamins and the moisture in the carrot itself. Store carrots refrigerated in a sealed plastic bag and not too close to apples or pears as they will start to taste bitter. In case you were wondering, baby carrots are simply smaller carrots that have been mechanically trimmed and peeled. Eating brown rice is also an excellent way to lower your high glycemic index, thus lowering your blood sugar levels.	Carrots are loaded with vitamins A, C and K. They are also rich in alpha, beta carotene, and fiber, which are all helpful in fighting cancer and vision loss.

PRODUCE	BENEFIT	VITAMINS & MINERALS
Flax Seed	Useful in lowering cholesterol and fighting some cancers. Many women have found relief from menopausal discomfort by taking a daily dose of flax seed oil. The fats found in flax seed oil may also help with joint pain and arthritis related inflammation. Whole flax seeds stay fresh at room temperature for a year or more. Ground flax seed stays good for up to four months. Unopened flax seed oil can be stored at room temperature. After opening, it can be stored in the refrigerator for up to six weeks.	A fantastic source of vitamins and minerals like thiamine, manganese and the heart-healthy omega-3 fatty acids.
Fish	How can you tell farm-raised salmon from the wild variety? Wild salmon meat is naturally pink. Farm-raised salmon has gray flesh. In order to give farm-raised salmon a pink coloring, some farmers add dye to the salmon.	Fish such as salmon and other fatty types such as mackerel and trout contains omega-3 fatty acids. These acids aid in protecting your brain, eyesight, heart, and assist in preventing some forms of cancers. Salmon is loaded with protein, and is a good source of vitamins B12, B6, niacin and selenium.
Garlic	Garlic kills bacteria, viruses, and infectious fungi. There have been some studies to suggest that garlic may improve high blood pressure and hardening of the arteries. If you take blood thinning, heart, and heart-related medications, please check with your doctor before adding garlic to your diet. When choosing garlic, select plump bulbs with dry skin. Avoid spongy, soft, or shriveled cloves. Also avoid purchasing garlic from the refrigerated section of the grocery store. Moisture spoils garlic. Unpeeled garlic heads can be stored in a dark, dry, cool place for up to two months. If stored in the refrigerator, use within three days.	Garlic has been proven to possess anti-infection properties.
Greens: Collard, Mustard, Turnip, and Kale	All varieties of greens are good for your eyes and they provide cataract protection. Greens are also heart-smart. The nutrients lutein and vitamin K that these leafy green vegetables contain are believed to help prevent heart attacks. When you add oil to your pot of greens, you help your body absorb the vitamin K.	An excellent source of fiber, vitamin E, folate, calcium, copper, manganese, and beta carotene. They also provide doses of vitamins A, C, and K.

PRODUCE	BENEFIT	VITAMINS & MINERALS
Peaches	Peaches are classified into three basic categories: 1) Free-stone-ripe, 2) Semi-freestone, and 3) Freestone. A common category known as Cling Stone-ripe peaches are available May through August. They are juicer and sweeter than the other two types of peaches and are used mostly for canning. Freestone-ripe peaches are available May through October. They tend to be larger, less juicy and tenderer than the Cling stone and are considered to be "eating" peaches. Semi-Freestone is a hybrid of the Cling Stone and Freestone. Look for peaches that are firm, but will yield with gentle pressure.	Peaches are a good source of potassium, and vitamins A and C.
Pears	There are several varieties: Anjou (mild and firm), Bartletts (juicy when raw, and loses shape when cooked), Bosc (crisp and grainy when raw, and will hold its shape when cooked), and Comice (great raw with a less grainy texture).	Pears are a good source of vitamin C and fiber.
Pomegranate	The fruit and juice offers the highest level of antioxidants of all fruit, although only the juice and seeds are edible. Pomegranate juice is loaded with polyphenols, which are known to inhibit cancer cell growth, slow tumor growth, and trigger cell death. The antioxidants concentrated in the pomegranate helps to protect the brain from damaging-free radicals. It is one of seven fruits that appear in the Bible's Old Testament.	High in vitamin C and potassium; pomegranate can protect your vision, battle heart disease, and assist with arthritis pain and memory loss.
Radish	Radish's greens are also edible. Radishes are divided into two categories: summer radishes, which are small and a vibrant, red, pink, purple, white, or red and white with flavor that goes from hot or mild. The other category is the winter radish such as daikon, which may be white, black, or green. Store summer radishes in plastic bags for up to a week, winter radishes for up to two weeks.	Provide potassium, vitamin C, folate and fiber. This is a good vegetable that helps detox the liver. Try eating each day whenever you have sinus or mucus issues
Winter Squash	Consists of acorn, butternut, the hubbard, and summer varieties. Look for squash that is compact and feels heavy with thick, clean skin.	Varieties of squash are a rich source of vitamins A and C, fiber, and potassium. They are also a good source of thiamine and folate.

A WORD OF CAUTION: DO NOT EAT SEEDLESS FRUITS AND VEGETABLES!
Do not eat produce that cannot reproduce it self.

REFERENCES:
Editors of FC&A Medical Publishing. Your Body Can Heal Itself, Over 87 Foods Everyone Should Eat. Peacetree City, Georgia:FC&A Publishing, 2008.
Bond, Annie, Breyer, Melissa, Gordon, Wendy and Waters, Alice. True Food 8 Simple Steps to a Healthier You. Washington, D.C.:National Geographic Books, 2010.

CHAPTER 8

Stocking Your Kitchen - Develop an Open Mind

My parents were from Alabama, but my brother, sister and I grew up in New Jersey. We always had apple cider vinegar and baking soda among the items stocked in our kitchen. My friends knew that if they wanted a good home-cooked meal and a big pot of greens, our house was the place to be. We should encourage each other to create a healthy kitchen that is a place of good health and fellowship.

You may not be familiar with some of the following items, but I highly recommend that you do a little research to understand their benefits. If we understand how to stock our kitchen, food can be used as "medicine".

ORGANIC VERSES CONVENTIONAL PRODUCE

My experience has been that organic produce typically tastes better and is better for our overall health.

Healthy, clean food is not to be taken for granted. The increase use of pesticides on produce has caused numerous health concerns. According to an article on the Grace Communication Foundation site, the top vegetables that contain the highest levels of pesticide are apples, celery, sweet bell peppers, peaches, strawberries, grapes, spinach, lettuce, cucumbers, blueberries, and potatoes.

This information was compiled by USDA & FDA data.*Environmental Working Group (2012) EWG 2012 Shoppers Guide to Pesticides in Produce.

Conventionally grown food is typically treated with pesticides. Organic food is typically non-genetically modified food without the use of chemical pesticides. There are natural methods used to grow food and avoid insects and fungus. Be careful when buying soybean and corn products. Use them sparingly and make sure you purchase organically grown soy beans and corn. According to the USDA, organically grown food is often fresher, has fewer pesticides, and is better for the environment.

Many urban communities have recognized the need to grow their own produce and become more food independent. This is a good approach to taking back control of our own environment and food. We must become more informed about the food we purchase and eat.

Many countries are much more informed about their food choices. In much of our travel overseas, we have found the food to be fresher and much more tasteful. Many of these countries continue to practice organic gardening.

Many people have told me that buying organic produce is more expensive. However, there are many farmers' markets that offer organic produce and grocery stores that offer sales on organic fruits and vegetables. Starting your own garden or partnering with neighbors to begin community gardening are choices to feed your family. I hope you are inspired to make better food purchases and monitor what you allow in your bodies. If we take the best care of our bodies and minds I believe God will help fill in the gaps. We should not be apathetic about our bodies. We were meant to last, but it has to be intentional. The quality of living is as important as the length of living. Being able to move and enjoy the blessing of family, nature, and new experiences enriches and our loved ones.

Please consider having as many of the following ingredients in your kitchen. If your budget is limited, add to the following suggestions as your dollars dictate. Also, make sure you look for sales in health food store and farmers markets.

CHAPTER 9

The Pantry

- **Sea salt**: There are several varieties of Sea salt. Unlike iodized salt, also known as regular table salt, sea salt still has minerals intact.

- **Olive, macadamia, safflower, and sesame oils:** These oils are better for the heart than other commonly used oils, and they assist with lowering high cholesterol.

- **Bragg® Organic Raw Unfiltered Apple Cider Vinegar** (or other unfiltered vinegars): This product is one of my cooking secrets. For example, add a tablespoon to your coleslaw dressing and you won't need as much mayo! It also adds a very distinct flavor to many dishes, and can even be used as a salad dressing. I prefer to use the Bragg's brand. This vinegar has many health benefits. It can be used as a tonic to maintain the body's pH balance. If you want to limit mucus in your system, this is a good addition. It has been beneficial in a weight loss program when used along with exercise and a healthy diet. If you have a sore throat, vinegar mixed with plain water is a helpful gargle. Also, if your muscles are sore and you're in need of a good rest, take a 20-minute bath. Add to the bath water one cup of apple cider vinegar and one cup of Epsom Sslt. (Refer to my book list: Apple Cider Vinegar by Patricia and Paul Bragg if you're interested in learning more.)

- **Kukicha**: also known as Twig Tea, I find that this wonderful tasting tea relieves fatigue and helps to alkalize the body. You can enjoy this tea in the morning instead of coffee. It has a small amount of caffeine, but it is pleasant tasting and gives you a little lift.

- **Red or Brown Miso Paste**: This paste is great to use when making vegetable soups. Miso has a lot of healing properties. If you have high blood pressure, make sure you are aware of the sodium content. I make this soup for my daughter whenever she has a fever or is a little under the weather. It really helps to settle the stomach, and it contains lots of nutrients. This product is very good for the intestines.

- **Umeboshi Plum Tea**: People with ulcers have found this tea to be helpful. It helps detoxify the liver (if you are congested you may want to drink this as a tea). This was a constant in my diet when I went through my healing phase in order to conceive.

- **Organic Brown Rice**: Try eating this instead of white rice. Brown rice has the minerals and fiber still intact. If you are a diabetic, this is a much better choice than white rice. It is a complex carbohydrate, which means it slowly breaks down in the digestive system. There are both long and short grain varieties available to purchase.

- **Turbinado** (also known as raw sugar), **pure maple syrup, and barley Syrup**: Instead of white sugar try these natural sweeteners.

- **Whole-Grain Flour**: White flour, like white rice, has been stripped of many of its nutrients. So, try other whole varieties such as wheat, spelt, and oat.

- **Steel Cut Oats**: This has a chewy texture and maintains higher fiber content. My family prefers to eat this type of oatmeal instead of rolled oats.

- **Kudzu**: This is made from a starchy root and is used to thicken sauces, stews, and pudding. It renews energy, relieves upset stomachs, and helps with controlling diarrhea.

- **Onions and garlic**: Always keep onions and garlic in the pantry. These items not only provide great flavor, but they also provide antioxidants and have bacteria fighting properties. Onions are a great vegetable to use for flavoring soups, stews, and other vegetables.

- **Aduki** - This is a bean that is easy to digest, helps energy, and is great for the skin.

- **Navy or white beans**: These beans contain many nutrients and lots of fiber.

- **Black-eyed peas**: These peas have many nutrients, and they assist with helping the body in producing amino acids.

- **Lentils**: There are several varieties of lentils, and they have many nutrients and are easy to digest; they are known to help combat heart disease and cancer.

CHAPTER 10

The Spice Rack

- **Bragg® Liquid Aminos Spray:** This spray is a delicious all-purpose soy protein spray that provides a salty taste without being high in sodium. All you need is one or two sprays for seasoning.

- **Bay leaves:** I use this seasoning in my purple hull peas, black-eyed peas, navy beans, and soups. It provides a wonderful flavor. Bay leaves are known to help the digestive system, especially combating flatulence. Caution: Be sure to remove the leaf after cooking. Do not eat the leaves; they are hard, so they could become damaging to your intestinal walls.

- **Ginger root** and **powder ginger:** Both forms of ginger are great seasonings for fish, chicken, and all types of vegetables. Ginger can be used in the raw root form by chopping or grating, or used in a powder form. Fresh grated ginger is great on salads, steamed broccoli, cauliflower, sautéed carrots, and in beans or soups. If you use the fresh root, do not place in boiling water because that limits its many healing properties. Ginger promotes circulation, alleviates congestion, helps the digestive system, and is a good boost to the immune system against colds. Many women also find relief from menstrual cramps by drinking ginger tea.

- **Paprika:** This is a mild seasoning that can add a dash of color and flavor to your dish. I add paprika to my fish, coleslaw, and potato salad dishes. Paprika is mild on the stomach and has been known to help with circulation.

- **Parsley:** In its dried form, parsley is great on fish and poultry. I love to use the fresh parsley in my soups and beans. This herb is good for digestion and packs many nutrients. Fresh parsley can be used as a natural breath freshener and to make a nice presentation during special family meals. Using parsley as a garnish helps to visually make foods more appealing. Your food should be not only attractive to the taste buds, but also to the eye.

- **Pure Vanilla Extract:** This is a great flavoring for puddings and other desserts; you can also use it when mixing fruit smoothies.

- **Cumin Seed:** This spice is delicious in bean recipes that include chili and all taco recipes. Cumin seeds and powder have many health benefits. They contain high amounts of iron and, when used frequently, are known for increasing bone density, protecting memory loss and many other benefits.

THE REFRIGERATOR
- Lemons
- Ginger Root
- Bragg's Apple Cider Vinegar
- Onions
- Organic broccoli (this can last at least a week)
- Organic carrots
- Organic romaine Lettuce (if stored properly, this remains fresh for approximately five days)

THE FREEZER
- Organic frozen vegetables and beans

Some of these items can be found in your local grocery store. Any well-stocked health food store will carry the other products. Depending on your health condition, gradually buy the products that may best meet your physical needs and satisfy your taste buds.

CHAPTER 11

The Importance of Healthy Cooking Oils

Think of your body as a smooth running machine that must stay lubricated. It is essential that we understand the importance of healthy fat in our diets. Think of good fats as lubricant for your arteries. I encourage you to search information based on the writings from the American Heart Association® and Mayo Clinic. Choose oils high in poly-unsaturated fats and mono-saturated fats. You can ensure that you are choosing the correct oil by reading the ingredient label.

We need to incorporate not only high quality foods, but also high quality fats. I particularly like olive oil, safflower oil, and sesame seed oil for stove-top cooking, and macadamia and coconut oils for baking. However, there are other high-quality oils such as, almond and avocado. You should choose oils that are low in saturated fat. Flaxseed oil can be beneficial for several physical ailments. It can be used in salad dressings, taken in a pill form, or as a liquid from a bottle. I choose not to use canola oil, as every oil except canola can be traced back to its source.

If you are on a tight budget, I recommend you start with safflower oil. It tends to be closer in the price range of regular vegetable oil. If you can, consider buying olive oil. And, if you must fry, try using safflower or coconut oil. It gives foods a nice light flavor. However, limit the fried foods as much as possible. If you are in good health and exercise consistently, you can treat yourself to fried foods on occasion.

In our home, I use Earth Balance Brand™ spread instead of butter or margarine. It is non-hydrogenated, which means it won't clog the arteries. This brand has several different versions. I use the one that doesn't contain canola oil. It has a great buttery taste, so it can be used in all of your baking recipes. At times, I also use it for my pie crusts and biscuit recipes. Try using it as a substitute, and let me know how you like the outcome. Remember this is about enjoying your food without killing yourself, so be open-minded.

As a rule of thumb, oils have a relative short self life. Depending on how long oil has been exposed to light, heat, and oxygen, oils generally last for six months to a year before going rancid. Cooking oils that are lighter in color have a longer shelf life than oils that are darker in color.

Just as all cooking oils are not created equal, not all cooking oils can be used for the same purposes. Due to each oil's smoke point, it is important to know which oils are better used for baking versus frying. The list below is a helpful guide.

BROWNING, SEARING, SAUTÉING, AND FRYING

- Almond
- Avocado
- Coconut
- Hazelnut
- High-oleic sunflower
- Safflower

BAKING, COOKING IN THE OVEN, AND STIR-FRYING

- Coconut
- Grape seed
- Macadamia
- Peanut
- Sesame
- Walnut

MARINADES, DRESSINGS, AND DIPS

- Extra Virgin olive oil (not recommended for use with heat or high temperatures)
- Flaxseed
- Wheat Germ (keep refrigerated)

CHAPTER 12

Choosing the Best Cookware

The type of cookware that we select is just as important as the type of foods that we choose to prepare. It has been reported most Americans have chemicals in their blood stream commonly associated with non-stick cookware, such as Teflon. I always caution not to use non-stick cookware. Be aware that when Teflon is cracked or scratched it can prove to be hazardous to your health. When Teflon is heated around 500 degrees Fahrenheit, breathing its fumes is unsafe. Its fumes can cause flu-like symptoms including chills, fever, cough, and headaches. Birds are especially sensitive to the fumes emitted by Teflon. The compounds found in non-stick cookware have been associated with inflated cholesterol levels in teens and children and osteoarthritis in adults.

When cooking, it is important to understand how food reacts with some of the metals and plastics commonly found in cookware. Foods high in acid, such as most fruits, tomatoes, lemon juice, and vinegar, react with cookware such as aluminum, unlined copper, and cast iron that has not been seasoned well. This reaction can leave food grayish in color with an unpleasant metallic taste. Some studies suggest an association of the use of aluminum cookware with Alzheimer's disease and other health problems.

Fats, such as chicken fat quickly absorb polymers found in plastics. Silicon appears to be the exception. As a rule, avoid microwaving and storing foods in plastic containers. Studies have shown that the poly-vinyl chloride (PVC) found in plastic wrap pose as health risks when it is in contact with food. PVC leaches DEAH, a hormone-disrupting toxin. It can damage the liver, lungs, and body tissues. Also, avoid plastics containing the toxic bisphenol-a (BPAs).

I SUGGEST USING THE FOLLOWING TYPES OF COOKWARE:
- **Cast Iron**: It conducts heat evenly, consistently, and is nonreactive. If well-seasoned, it is non-stick. Do not use when preparing all-day tomato sauces. Cast iron can be used both on the cooktop and in the oven. See the instructions below for seasoning your skillet. This is one of the best cookware for growing children and women before menopause. However, this may not be the best cookware for men or menopausal women. Iron leaks into food, which is good if you need iron but harmful if you do not. It can cause fatigue, impotence, arthritis, and a number of other health issues, so please us wisely.

- **Ceramic and Earthenware**: Both are nonreactive to heat and agents. They are great for recipes that call for baking and simmering. Do not cook with antique or cookware labeled "or design or decorative purposes only" or "not for food use." Some ceramics may be glazed with unsafe pigments that contain cadmium or lead. Avoid using any cookware if you are unsure if it is lead free. If a gray powder appears on the glaze, do not use it.

- **Stainless Clad Steel**: The cladding of the steel makes this cookware nonreactive. The suggested weight to purchase is surgical steel or heavy-gauge. It heats evenly. Take care not to scratch the surface when stirring or scouring. The metal underneath can leach into food and possibly present health issues.

- **Enamel-Coated Cast Iron and Bake ware**: Enamel is a layered-fused glass, sometimes called porcelain. It conducts heat evenly. It can be used on top of the stove and in the oven. If the enamel layer chips, the pot should be thrown away. The enamel can break off into the food exposing the metal underneath to whatever you are cooking. Quality enamelware should last for quite some time.

- **Glass**: It is nonreactive and safe to use, but it tends to conduct heat unevenly. Glass is excellent for mixing and storing food. Glass is also rust free.

- **Silicone**: This material is nonreactive. This synthetic rubber is used as non-stick bake ware. Below 428 degrees Fahrenheit, it is heat resistant.

- **Bamboo**: This material is nonreactive. It is especially useful when used as steamers, crockery and utensils.

SEASONING YOUR CAST IRON SKILLET
1. Place a sheet of aluminum foil on the bottom rack of your oven to catch drips.
2. Preheat your oven to 450 degrees Fahrenheit.
3. If your cast iron skillet is new, you must first wash off the factory anti-rust coating with a mild detergent and hot water.
4. Dry by heating the skillet on the cook top.
5. Allow the skillet to cool.
6. Rub the skillet with a vegetable oil such as sunflower or coconut oil.
7. Heat the skillet in the oven for 30 minutes. There will be some smoke.
8. Allow the skillet to cool in the oven to room temperature.

REFERENCES:
1Kim E. Innes, Alan M. Ducatman, Michael I. Luster, Anoop Shankar, " Association of Osteoarthritis With Serum Levels of the Environmental Contaminants Perfluorooctanoate and Perfluorooctane Sulfonate in a Large Appalachian Population," American Journal of Epidemiology (March 8, 2011). 2Sarah S. Knox, Timothy Jackson, Beth Javins, Stephanie J. Frisbee, Anoop Shankar and Alan M. Ducatman, "Implications of Early Menopause in Women Exposed to Perfluorocarbons," Journal of Endocrinology and Metabolism (February 23, 2011). 3Cheryl R. Stein, David A. Savitz, "Serum Perfluorinated Compound Concentration and Attention Deficit/Hyperactivity Disorder in Children 5–18 Years of Age," Environmental Health Perspectives (October 2011).
4Jane Muncke, "Endocrine Disrupting Chemicals and Other Substances of Concern in Food Contact Materials: An Updated Review of Exposure, Effect and Risk Assessment," The Journal of Steroid Biochemistry and Molecular Biology 127 (October 2011): 118-127. 5Sarah, Healthy Living, the Healthy Home Economist, The Health Hazards of Cast Iron Pans

APPLES & BERRIES FRUIT SALAD – *A family favorite*

This is a delicious refreshing quick breakfast. I highly recommend organic fruit.
Quantities can be adjusted based on the number of servings.

Servings: 2 to 3
Prep time: 10 minutes
Difficulty: Easy

Ingredients:
Sliced apples (or pears in the fall)
Handful of blueberries or strawberries
2 to 3 tbsp of soy or non dairy yogurt (your favorite flavor)
3 tbsp of high-quality granola (use low-fat and low-sugar variety)
Dash of cinnamon

Directions:
Wash all of the fruit thoroughly.
Spoon the sliced fruit and berries into a bowl and then add the yogurt.
Stir, add cinnamon, top with granola and serve.

EATING CEREALS WITH PLANT MILKS

Try eating whole grain cereals with less than 10 grams of sugar per serving. Instead of eating cereal with diary milk, try it with almond, coconut, oat, or soy milk. If you don't like the taste, try another brand. I prefer Silk®, Eden® or the Dream® brands.

STEEL CUT OATS *(with cinnamon)*

Steel Cut Oats have much higher fiber content than other oats. They are packed with protein and other nutrients (you don't always need meat to get your protein). Prepare according to the instructions on the package but try adding a little more water and let it cook at least 15 minutes. Make sure while it is cooking, you stir the oats several times. This will make the cereal creamier. It has a nutty taste and is very satisfying. Add a dash a cinnamon to make it taste great! Also, try a teaspoon of pure maple syrup instead of the usual sugar…and, please skip the butter.

I suggest having a cup of green tea with lemon, honey, pure maple syrup, raw turbinado sugar or agave (if diabetic) in the morning to accompany your oatmeal.

Follow directions on box according to desired servings.

WINTER CREAM OF FARINA

This is a delicious warm cereal recipe created by my dear daughter, Abeni Jewel. This is a quick cereal recipe that most could make before leaving for school.

Servings: 2
Prep Time: According to the box instructions
Difficulty: Easy

Ingredients:
 2 cups almond milk or other plant-based milk
 1/3 cup Farina (Cream of Wheat)
 ¼ tsp. Sea Salt
 1 tsp. pure vanilla extract
 ½ tsp. nutmeg
 ½ ginger
 ½ cinnamon
 2 tbsp. maple syrup

Directions:
Prepare the farina according to the directions on the box, using almond milk instead of water. Add the seasonings and maple syrup as soon as Farina thickens. Stir and serve.

This should make 2 healthy servings.

CHAPTER 14
Quick Dinner Suggestions

VEGETARIAN STIR-FRY

This recipe can be altered by changing vegetables. Be creative. I'd like to introduce kudzu, which is one of those wonderful plants that can provide both food and medicine. Kudzu contains compounds called isoflavones, commonly known as antioxidants, because of its ability to trap singlet oxygen. When eaten, there are indications that there is a lower incidence of certain cancers. As food, it is a great ingredient to create sauces for stir-fry dishes. The leaves can be consumed or the root can be ground into a powder that's better than cornstarch because of the smooth texture without a starchy taste or bitterness. Kudzu is used widely in the macrobiotic diet because it helps with digestive problems. Many of us would be much healthier if we had better functioning digestive systems. One small bag of this product will last for several months. You can purchase kudzu at most health food stores.

Servings: 3
Prep Time: 10 to 15 minutes
Cooking Time: Approximately 15 minutes (not including the brown rice, prepare according to package)
Difficulty: Easy Recipe

If you have more people, add additional vegetables and rice. The brown rice is very filling.

Ingredients:
   2 cups of shitake mushrooms (this satisfies the need for protein; you can also use tofu or organic or vegetarian chicken)
   2 large organic carrots, washed, peeled, and chopped
   ½ medium organic yellow onion, chopped
   3 to 5 organic kale leaves washed, stems removed, and chopped; or sliced cabbage
   3 tbsp of safflower oil
   1 tbsp of kudzu dissolved in about one cup of cold water
   1 tbsp of dried organic parsley
   1 tsp of organic basil
   2 organic garlic cloves smashed
   Sea salt to taste or Braggs Amino Acid Spray
   Brown rice (long or short grain prepare according to package directions)
   In the winter months, add a teaspoon of oregano or dried rosemary. These herbs tend to help warm the body

Vegetarian Stir-Fry (continued)

Directions:

In a large stainless steel pan, add oil over medium heat.

Add chopped onion and smashed garlic. Sauté until the onions are almost translucent.

Add the shitake mushrooms (or other protein), and sauté until almost thoroughly cooked.

Add the remaining ingredients and seasonings, cover for about 5 minutes.

Add the cup of dissolved kudzu to the pan and lightly stir until the kudzu thickens; it provides the sauce for the stir fry (read label for preparation).

Adjust the seasonings to taste.

Pour over prepared brown rice and serve.

VEGGIE BURGER DINNER

Servings: According to the box
Prep time: According to the box instructions
Difficulty: Easy

Use the best veggie patty (one that has quality ingredients) and check the sodium content on the pack. Prepare according to directions on the label.

Place the patty on a whole-grain bun and prepare as you would a hamburger with all the fixings.

Add a green salad made with romaine or another dark leafy lettuce and you have a quick meal.

VEGETARIAN FISH TACOS
A family favorite

Use your typical taco recipe; however make a few changes to make it healthier. Instead of beef, try using ground veggie meat, beans, fish, or ground turkey. To save money, try using chili powder instead of taco seasoning packs. I learned this trick to limit sodium in the dish when I discovered that I didn't have taco seasoning!

Servings: 8 to12 tacos
Prep Time: Approximately 15 minutes
Cook Time: Approximately 15 minutes
Difficulty: Easy

Ingredients:

    1 8 oz pkg of veggie ground meat or 2 medium white fish fillets*
    ½ chopped organic onion
    ½ chopped organic green pepper
    2 to 3 tbsp chili powder
    ½ tsp garlic powder
    3 sliced organic romaine lettuce leaves
    ½ chopped organic tomato
    ½ chopped veggie, American or cheddar cheese
    2 tbsp of safflower or olive oil
    1 small or medium size jar of organic salsa

Directions:

Sauté onion and green peppers over medium heat until they are slightly done. Add the veggie meat and cook well by mixing the meat with vegetables. I usually sprinkle a little water over the top to steam the sodium out of the mixture.

If I make a dozen tacos, I use 2 to 3 tablespoons of chili powder dissolved in a half cup of warm water. Make sure you stir the powder well and then add to the meat just as you normally would. Let it simmer until the water has almost evaporated, but the meat isn't dry.

Spoon the seasoned mixture into the taco shells, add shredded lettuce, then tomatoes, non-dairy cheese (find the best brand for you), and a tablespoon of salsa.

* To prepare the fish fillets, use a cast iron skillet or stainless steel pan. Lightly oil the pan with safflower oil. Lightly season the fish with sea salt and white pepper. On medium heat, sauté the fish until the fillets are fully cooked but not dry. This process should take approximately 10 minutes, depending on the thickness of the fish. After the fish has fully cooked, take the spatula and lightly chop up the fish. Spoon the fish into the shells and proceed as above.

———————————————————————————

DEB'S 2-BEAN VEGGIE CHILI

Servings: 3 to 5
Prep Time: Approximately 10 minutes
Cook Time: Approximately 20 minutes
Difficulty: Easy

Ingredients:

1 pkg of ground veggie meat (read the package: the fewer ingredients the better)
½ large yellow onion, chopped
½ medium green pepper, chopped
1 can or carton of organic kidney beans*
1 can or carton of organic black beans
1-8 oz jar of mild salsa
2 tbsp of safflower oil
1 tbsp chili powder
2 peeled and chopped garlic cloves
1 tbsp dried parsley
½ tsp oregano
Sea salt to taste

Directions:

Place safflower oil in a medium sauce pan on medium low heat. Sauté' until onions and green peppers are slightly cooked. Add veggie ground meat and sauté until fully cooked. Drain half of the bean juice from each can — or if you want a thicker chili, drain all of the juice — and add to the sautéed ingredients. Heat the ingredients thoroughly. Add the salsa and all of the remaining seasonings. Cover and simmer on low heat for approximately 15 minutes. Taste and make salt adjustments if needed.

*There are a few canning companies, like Eden Foods, that have taken the lead (BPA) out of their cans. Please read the labels. I prefer to avoid canned foods when possible and use the new pouches or cartons that some companies offer.

Please choose a brand with the lowest sodium content.

CHAPTER 15
Pasta Dishes

ANGEL HAIR PASTA WITH FISH SAUTÉ

Please don't be intimidated by the list of ingredients. This dish does not take much time to prepare and cook – and it's colorful and tasty. Add a fresh salad or sautéed greens to complete this meal.

Servings: 5 to 6
Prep Time: Approximately 15 minutes
Cook Time: Approximately 15 minutes
Difficulty: Medium

Ingredients:

    8 oz box of whole grain or whole wheat angel hair or spaghetti pasta
    6 oz of fresh white fish (Rainbow Trout and Tilapia works well)
    3 to 4 tbsp of fresh parsley
    1 crushed garlic clove
    1 tsp of capers
    2 tbsp of safflower oil
    ½ onion, grated
    1 tbsp of kudzu powder*
    1 cup of cold water
    1 tsp of powder ginger
    ½ tsp white pepper
    Sea salt to taste

Directions:

Prepare the pasta according to the directions on the box. Heat the sauce pan on medium-heat.

In a stainless steel pan, sauté parsley, onions, and garlic in the safflower oil for about 5 minutes until you can smell the delicious aroma. Make sure you that you use a spatula and lightly stir the ingredients.

Add the fresh fish and cover the pan for about 5 to 8 minutes until the fish is almost completely cooked. Take the spatula and lightly chop the fish. If the fish is difficult to chop it may not be cooked enough. It should be light and flaky.

Dissolve kudzu powder in a cup of cold water. Add to the fish sauté and make sure that the heat is on medium low. In a few minutes the kudzu liquid will turn transparent. Turn heat on low and add the remainder of the seasonings.

Pour over paste and serve.

Kudzu powder is used to thicken sauces, soups and puddings. This is a powder from a plant; it is good for the digestive system.

SOULFUL VEGETARIAN MACARONI AND CHEESE
Servings: 4
Prep Time: Approximately 45 minutes
Cook Time: Approximately 10 minutes
Difficulty: Easy

Ingredients:
    1 8 oz box of spelt or regular macaroni
    ½ package of rice, soy or almond shredded cheese (American or cheddar flavor)
    2 tbsp of Earth Balance Buttery Spread
    ½ cup of rice, soy or almond milk
    1/4 tsp of sea salt
    Dash of white pepper

Directions:
Preheat oven to 350 degrees Fahrenheit.

Prepare the macaroni product according to the box directions.

In a sauce pan, heat milk over medium low heat and add shredded cheese and Earth Balance. Stir the mixture until cheese is almost melted, add salt and white pepper.

Place cooked macaroni in an oven ready bowl.

Pour the melted cheese mixture over the macaroni; slightly stir to make sure all of the macaroni is covered. Bake for approximately 10 minutes.

Sprinkle paprika over the macaroni for an inviting presentation.

NOODLES AND MUSHROOMS

The soba noodles contain protein and fiber. The shitake mushrooms are high in nutrients, and can be used in place of meat because of its high protein content.

Servings: 4
Prep Time: Approximately 10 minutes
Cook Time: Approximately 15 minutes
Difficulty: Easy

Ingredients:
   1 8 oz pkg of soba noodles or spaghetti whole grain noodles
   1 cup of chopped shitake mushrooms (remove the stems)
   ¼ cup chopped onion
   1 tsp parsley
   ½ tsp white pepper
   Sea salt to taste
   Garlic powder to taste
   2 tsp of kudzu powder
   1 tsp safflower oil

Directions:
Prepare the package noodles according to the directions, drain and set to one side.

In a small sauté pan or stainless steel pan, pour oil and lightly cook the mushrooms over low medium heat, stirring frequently for approximately 5 minutes.

Lightly salt and add a dash of garlic and pepper to the mushrooms.

Dissolve the kudzu in ½ cup of water and add to the noodles. Return noodles to the heat for a few minutes, until the liquid turns clear.

Add the mushrooms, parsley, salt and pepper and lightly toss.

CREAMY TUNA CASSEROLE

This dish should be eaten occasionally to warm the stomach, particularly during chilly weather. I prefer spelt macaroni because it is much lighter tasting than some other brands. Serve with a green salad to complete your meal.

Servings: 4 to 5
Prep Time: Approximately 10 minutes
Cook Time: Approximately 35 to 40 minutes
Difficulty: Easy

Ingredients:
 1 8 oz box of organic Vita spelt macaroni or your favorite brand
 1 tbsp of safflower oil
 1 can of tuna (fished responsibly) or 6 oz of fresh cooked tuna
 4 to 5 slices of rice, almond, or soy cheese (American or cheddar flavor)
 ½ yellow onion chopped or grated
 1 tbsp of Earth Balance® spread
 ½ cup of almond, oat, or soy milk (rice milk may not be heavy enough)
 1 tsp of dried parsley
 1 2.2 oz can of black olives (optional)
 Sea salt and white pepper to taste
 Paprika

Directions:
Preheat oven to 350 degrees Fahrheit.

In a medium size stainless steel pot, prepare the macaroni according to the instructions on the box. Do not overcook the macaroni. Remove just before the suggested time because you will place the macaroni in the oven and you want to maintain its form.

Drain any excess water by pouring the macaroni through a strainer placed on the pot.

In a separate small pan, add safflower oil and lightly sauté the onion. Cut cheese into strips and add to the macaroni and stir.

Add sautéed onion and seasonings. Pour almond, oat, or soy milk over macaroni.

Add Earth Balance® and lightly stir all ingredients together in the pot until the cheese begins to melt. Make sure that the tuna is flaked before you add it to the mixture.

Then add the olives and lightly fold into the mixture.

Pour the mixture in a casserole dish and sprinkle with paprika. Paprika makes a nice presentation, which is also good for the appetite.

Bake for approximately 10 minutes to allow the mixture to settle. Remove from the oven and let sit for a few minutes before serving.

QUICK SALMON PASTA SALAD

Servings Approximately 3
Preparation Time: Approximately 10 minutes
Difficulty: Easy

Ingredients:

1 can salmon
1 cup cooked brown rice pasta
1 or 2 tablespoons of grated onions
1 chopped celery stalk
2 tablespoons high quality Mayonnaise
2 teaspoons Debra's Bean Blend
White Pepper to Taste
Sea Salt to Taste

Directions:

In a medium bowl, use a fork to flake the salmon. Mix in grated onions, chopped celery stalk and cooked pasta. Add all the seasonings and stir with fork until blended. Add mayonnaise and remainder of the seasonings and blend. Debra's Bean Blend will give this dish a unique delicious taste and add color.

Eat on a bed a romaine lettuce or as a scoop on top of a green tossed salad. This recipe should accommodate 3 servings.

CHAPTER 16

Fish Selections

There are two main categories of fish: oily and white. Oily fish is higher in fat than white fish, but it contains more polyunsaturated fat, which is a good fat and a great source of omega 3 fatty acids. Omega 3 is vital to the body for growth and development of the brain and nervous system. It can also help to reduce levels of cholesterol in the blood. Cholesterol is a bad fat and is often associated with increased risk of stroke and heart disease. It can affect the arteries, causing them to narrow or become blocked and potentially trigger a heart attack. Recent scientific studies have suggested that oily fish are particularly beneficial to the health of our hearts. As well as being a great source of vitamin D, they are also the best source of omega fatty acids, in particular omega 3. Because our bodies cannot produce omega fatty acids, it is vital that we get them from other sources. That's why having a balanced diet rich in fish and plant oil to give us omega 6 is so important. White fish is low in fat and high in protein. It also contains some omega 3 fatty acids, but not nearly as much as oily fish. I personally recommend white fish over oily fish. These tender fish fillets are delicious when cooked in a variety of ways. The white fish fillets are so tender that they fall apart with the touch of a fork. Due to concerns regarding lead content in tuna, I suggest limiting consumption to no more than three times per month. In my previous book, *The Beginner's Guide to Healthy Living*, I listed a few varieties of fish, but due to recent discoveries and news stories, I deleted many fish from the list. For example,. there have been numerous news stories regarding tilapia. Along with other varieties of fish, there has been more farm-raised fish due to the overfishing and pollution in our oceans. Please be cautious, ask questions about what the fish are fed. Some reports found tilapia farms fed fish pork scraps. Remember the saying, "Buyer Beware" when purchasing any type of fish. Below is a limited list of both oily and white fish.

OILY/FATTY FISH

Anchovies	Mackerel	Pacific Halibut	Trout
Herring	Salmon	Sardines	Tuna

WHITEFISH

Cod	Lemon sole	Red & grey mullet	Turbot
Flounder	Monkfish	Red Snapper	White fish
Haddock	Perch	Rock Salmon	Whiting
Halibut	Pickerel	Sea bass	
Hoki	Pollack	Shark	
John Dory	Red fish	Striped Bass	

BROILED FISH

This is a great alternative to fried foods because broiling can give the fish a nice crisp skin. Enjoy with a side of salad or other freshly prepared vegetable.

Servings: 1 medium fillet per person
Prep Time: Approximately 5 minutes
Cook Time: Approximately 10 minutes
Difficulty: Easy

Ingredients:
  Fish fillets
  Sea salt
  Powdered ginger
  White pepper

Directions:
Lightly wash the fillets with cold water and pat dry. Season fish fillets by sprinkling with sea salt, powdered ginger, and white pepper.

Place fillets in an oiled glass or stainless steel pan. Place the pan on a rack with the skin side down under broiler, and broil for approximately 5 to 6 minutes, depending on the thickness of the fillets

Turn fillets over and broil skin side up for another 5 to 6 minutes, remove and serve.

FISH SAUTÉ

Use the seasonings recommended above, and then add parsley by sprinkling it over each side of the fillets. Place the fish in a lightly oiled heated pan using safflower, coconut, walnut, or sesame oil. Cook each side for approximately 5 minutes.

SALMON SALAD DINNER

Salmon is an oily fish very rich in omega 3 fatty acids and is available fresh or canned. This particular recipe is one of the few times I recommend using a canned product.

Servings: 2
Prep Time: Approximately 10 minutes
Difficulty: Easy

Ingredients:

    1 4 oz can of pink salmon or 4 oz. broiled salmon steak

    ½ head of romaine lettuce (one whole head feeds approx. 4 people)

    1 tsp capers

    2 carrots washed, peeled and shredded

    Use red onions and any other fresh vegetable you desire in the salad

Directions:

Wash the lettuce and tear it into pieces. My mother always taught me to tear lettuce instead of cutting it so the nutrients will stay intact. Using a hand-held grater shred the carrots over the lettuce. Then, mix all the other desired fresh veggies into the salad.

Drain the canned salmon, break the meat into pieces and mix it into the salad. Top with ginger, sesame dressing, or vinaigrette.

Serve with whole grain or wheat, crackers or bread.

NOTE: If you increase the amount of lettuce and add another can of salmon, this quick dish could feed up to five people.

———————————————————

QUICK AND TASTY BAR-B-QUE SAUCE *for fish or poultry, no pork!*

Use this sauce occasionally on fish or poultry to give it an extra kick!

Servings: 2 medium fish fillets

Prep Time: Approximately 10 minutes

Difficulty: Easy

Ingredients:

    3 tbsp of agave sweetened ketchup

    2 tsp of horseradish mustard (I prefer Anne's Brand)

    ½ tsp of vegetarian Worcestershire sauce

    Increase each ingredient by a tablespoon to serve more

Directions:

Combine ingredients with a spoon and mix until well blended. Pour the sauce over grilled, sautéed or steamed fish. Cover and let steam for at least 5 minutes before serving.

CHAPTER 17

Simple Broths & Soups

VEGETABLE BROTH

When cooking greens, particularly collards and kale, make sure that you keep the stems stored in your refrigerator crisper to use to make broth. Broccoli stalks can also be used for broth.

This recipe is for a base to use when preparing soups and beans.

Prep Time: Approximately 10 minutes
Cook Time: Approximately 25 minutes
Difficulty: Easy

Ingredients:
   3 to 4 celery stalks
   5 to 6 collard or kale stalks
   ½ large yellow onion chopped
   1 tbsp of safflower oil
   1 inch of kombu seaweed that's been soaked for about 10 minutes
   Approximately 4 cups of high-quality water

Directions:
In a medium to large stainless steel or ceramic pot, over medium heat, pour water in the pot and bring it to a boil.

Place kombu, chopped greens stalks, onion and oil in the boiling water. Turn the heat down to low and allow vegetables to simmer until tender.

Using a stainless steel strainer, remove the vegetables by pouring the contents of the pot through the strainer. Pour the liquid into a bowl or another pot if you are going to use it immediately as a soup base or as a base for cooking beans.

BARLEY SOUP

Barley is an excellent whole grain to add to your weekly diet.

Servings: 3 to 4
Prep Time: Approximately 10 minutes
Cook Time: Approximately 2 hours (prepare barley according to package suggestions)
Difficulty: Easy

Ingredients:

   1/3 cup of pearled barley
   ½ package of organic frozen mixed vegetables
   1 cup of frozen baby lima beans
   3 to 4 cups of vegetable broth (see vegetable broth recipe)
   2 tbsp of safflower oil
   ½ tsp of white pepper
   2 tsp of dried or fresh parsley
   ½ tsp of dried or fresh basil
   1 tbsp of ketchup (agave sweetened is preferred)
   Sea salt to taste

Directions:

In a medium to large stainless steel pot, cook barley according to the package or 1 to 1 ½ hours in at least 3 cups of water. Loosely cover the pot.

After barley is almost completely cooked, add vegetable broth, safflower oil, vegetables and seasonings and let simmer for another 20 minutes.

Add ketchup and lightly stir. If needed, you may want to add a little water to keep the liquid the consistency of soup, and not a stew.

_____

LENTIL SOUP

Servings: 3 to 4
Prep Time: Approximately 15 minutes
Cook Time: Approximately 1 hour
Difficulty: Easy

Ingredients:

1 cup of red, green, or black lentils (red lentils have a faster cook time)
3 cups of water
½ chopped medium yellow onion
1 inch of Kombu seaweed (optional, it adds flavor and minerals to the soup)
About 3 chopped kale leaves
2 peeled and sliced carrots
2 cloves of garlic peeled and smashed
1 tsp of dried parsley
1 tsp of dried Italian herb combination (optional)
2 tbsp of safflower or olive oil
Sea salt to taste
White pepper

Directions:

Soak kombu in a cup of water for about 15 minutes. Rinse and place it in the bottom of a medium sauce pan.

Add lentils and water in a medium to large saucepan; bring to a boil for approximately 3 to 5 minutes. Lower heat to medium-low, and add vegetables and the garlic.

Add the oil, gently stir the ingredients, cover and simmer for about 20 minutes. Cover the saucepan for another 10 minutes. Add parsley, sea salt, and white pepper. Let simmer for another 5 minutes.

Serve with corn bread or quality crackers and a green salad.

FISH STEW

Fish stew is good for fall or winter dish.

This recipe doesn't take more than 45 minutes to prepare.

Servings: 4
Prep Time: Approximately 20 minutes
Cook Time: Approximately 20 minutes
Difficulty: Easy

Ingredients:

½ of chopped onion
½ of chopped green pepper
2 8 oz cans of organic tomatoes (no salt added)
2 cups of water
2 cloves of chopped garlic
2 fillets of white fish (Striped Bass, tilapia, trout, snapper, etc)
3 medium chopped red potatoes (this dish can also be prepared without potatoes)
½ pound of cleaned and deveined shrimp or fresh crab
½ cup fresh parsley
1 bay leaf (remove the leaf before serving – it is dangerous to swallow because it can puncture the intestines)
1 tbsp of fresh or dried basil
½ tsp of dried oregano
½ tsp of dried rosemary
2 tbsp of olive or safflower oil
Sea salt to taste
White pepper to taste

Directions:

Sauté onion, green pepper and garlic in oil over medium heat in a large sauce pan. Lightly season the fish fillets and add to the sautéed mix in the sauce pan.

Before adding other ingredients, lightly chop the fish with a spatula.

Add canned tomatoes, water, chopped potatoes with skin and bay leaf. Cover and simmer for approximately 10 to 12 minutes. From time to time, check to make sure that potatoes maintain their form but are also slightly soft.

Add the shrimp and remaining ingredients, cover and simmer on medium-low heat for another 5 to 8 minutes. Taste and sprinkle sea salt to your liking. Remember that seafood generally has a slightly salty taste, so you will have to watch your sodium content.

CHOWDERS

Try replacing milk or cream with cashew cream for your chowder recipes. Depending on the servings, soak one cup of raw unsalted cashews in cold water for a few hours. Drain the water and pour into a high speed blender. Begin on blend cycle and slowly drizzle water until cashews start to get creamy. Immediately stop adding water so the mixture will become thick and creamy. Make sure all cashews have been well blended. You may want to try the whipping cycle too. Slowly add this mixture to your chowder recipe as you would with the cream or milk. It is very rich, full of nutrients and combines well with your seasonings.

VEGETABLE TOFU STEW

This is a delicious and filling stew.

Servings: 4
Prep time: Approximately 20 minutes
Cook time: Approximately 40 minutes
Difficulty: Easy

Ingredients:

½ cup chopped onion
1 vegetarian kielbasa sausage link (links tend to have a high sodium content so only use 1)
2 cups vegetable broth (unsalted)
1 tablespoon safflower oil
2 chopped carrots
½ head organic cauliflower
2 medium red potatoes chopped
1 celery stalk chopped
½ pack firm organic tofu cut into cups
1 bay leaf
1 teaspoon garlic powder
½ teaspoon thyme
½ dried oregano
1 tablespoon dried parsley
8 oz. organic tomato sauce
Sea salt to Taste
White pepper to taste

Directions:

In a sauce pan, spread the safflower oil around the bottom of the pan. Turn stove top on medium-low and sauté onions with chopped vegetarian sausage and tofu until onions are translucent and sausage is slightly brown. Set aside off of heat. In a separate deeper sauce pan pour ½ cup of vegetable broth and heat on medium heat. Add chopped celery and cauliflower and sauté in vegetable broth until cauliflower is slightly soft. Don't overcook because you need vegetables to maintain a slight crunch.

Add carrots and all seasonings in the large sauce pan and stir. Add all the ingredients from the first sauce pan. Make sure you slightly scrape the bottom of the pan to release any of the sausage seasoning and add to the larger pan. Add the remaining vegetable broth, tomato sauce, and potatoes. Cook for at least 5 minutes on medium heat.

Then turn down on low heat and simmer for approximately 20 minutes. Let the stew stand at least 15 minutes before serving to allow seasoning to penetrate all ingredients. Serve with a salad or greens and good bread.

You don't need a lot of salt because salt is in the sausage and tomato sauce. Make sure you read the labels and buy the products with the least amount of sodium.

CHAPTER 19

Vegetable Sides

COLLARD GREENS

If greens are right out of the garden, you may have to wash them two to three times to remove any grit. I prefer to use alkaline water; however, if you do not possess an alkaline water machine, I suggest using a natural veggie and fruit spray to cleanse the vegetables. This process should not take more than 15 minutes, so don't let that be a deterrent.

Servings: 4
Prep Time: Approximately 15 to 20 minutes
Cook Time: Approximately 10 to 15 minutes
Difficulty: Easy

Ingredients:
    2 to 3 bunches of collard greens (or kale)
    1 large onion
    3 tbsp of safflower oil
    Peeled and crushed garlic clove, optional
    Sea salt and white pepper to taste
    Anaheim pepper or green pepper, optional

Directions:
Wash greens using veggie wash and water. Place greens in the sink and cover with water and spray once again with veggie wash. Make sure that all dirt is washed off of the leaves. Drain water and rinse again.

Hold leaves by the end of the stalk and slice the green leaves off of their stalks with a sharp knife, or tear if you prefer. Then, roll leaves and cut the leaves to about 1-inch slices. However, if you prepare kale I suggest you tear the leaves instead.

Select a medium to large pot and cover the bottom with 1 to 2 inches of water. Bring water to a boil.

Place sliced onion in the boiling water, along with the garlic. Add the sliced greens and oil.

Collard Greens *(continued)*

Cover pot, turn the heat down to medium low and cook for about 10 minutes. Stir the greens, onion and garlic so that all of the seasonings are thoroughly mixed. Cook for approximately 5 more minutes, maybe less.

Serve plain or with hot pepper sauce, southern chow chow, or sliced onions and tomatoes.

Kale greens can be cooked with the same recipe. Turnip and mustard greens should be washed with care; they can be prepared according to the above recipe. However, mustard and turnip greens cook best when not chopped but large hard stems are removed.

RACHEL'S CABBAGE
Servings: 4 to 5
Prep Time: Approximately 15 minutes
Cook Time: Approximately 10 minutes
Difficulty: Easy

Ingredients:
 1 head of green cabbage
 ½ thinly sliced medium onion
 ½ green pepper chopped
 3 tbsp safflower oil
 Sea salt
 White pepper
 1 to 2 cloves of garlic peeled and smashed

Directions:
After washing the cabbage, cut off the bottom stem of the cabbage. Slice the head of cabbage into four sections or cut it in half. You should be able to feed three people with half a head of cabbage.

Thinly slice the cabbage with a sharp knife and set to one side.

In a stainless steel pot or sauté pan, add oil and bring to medium heat. Sauté the sliced onion and green pepper with the garlic in the safflower oil for about 5 to 10 minutes (do not allow the onions to brown).

Add the sliced cabbage and sauté. You might want to add a little water because this will steam the cabbage. Cover and cook for about 8 minutes stirring at least once. Add sea salt and white pepper to taste.

The cabbage should be well cooked, but still crispy. This is another signature dish from my sweet godmother.

GREEN AND PURPLE CABBAGE SAUTÉ

Purple cabbage gives this dish a nice sweetness.

Servings: 4 to 5
Prep Time: Approximately 15 minutes
Cook Time: Approximately 10 minutes
Difficulty: Medium

Ingredients:
 ½ head of green cabbage
 ¼ head of purple cabbage
 ½ medium onion, thinly sliced
 2 tbsp of safflower oil
 1 tsp of garlic powder or 2 crushed and peeled garlic cloves
 White pepper
 Sea salt

Directions:
Wash cabbages and cut the heads in suggested sections as described in Rachel's Cabbage recipe.

In a medium to large stainless steel skillet, over medium heat, add safflower oil and then the onion. Sauté until the onions are almost translucent. Then add the cabbage and cover for about 5 minutes.

Add a dash of salt, white pepper, other seasonings and lightly sauté. Do not stir too much because it will cause the purple cabbage to bleed. Cover for another few minutes and serve.

———————————————————

GREEN (STRING) BEANS

Servings: 3 to 4
Prep Time: Approximately 10 minutes
Cook Time: Approximately 15 minutes
Difficulty: Easy

Ingredients:

½ pound of string beans
½ medium, chopped onion
2 tbsp olive or safflower oil
Cayenne pepper
Sea salt

Directions:

Wash the string beans and snap them in half. Make sure that you break off the steams. In a stainless steel pot, add about ¼ cup of clean water. Bring to a boil, add onion and cover for a few minutes. To the boiling water, add string beans and safflower oil. Cover for about 10 minutes. Lower heat and add sea salt and a dash of cayenne pepper. Stir and let simmer for another few minutes and serve.

———————————————————

BRUSSELS SPROUTS

Servings: 4 to 5
Prep Time: Approximately 10 minutes
Cook Time: Approximately 10 minutes
Difficulty: Easy

Ingredients:

1 pound of Brussels sprouts
2 to 3 tbsp of olive or safflower oil
½ tsp garlic powder
½ tsp sea salt
1 tbsp of water

Directions:

Wash and cut the Brussels sprouts in half, and sauté them in a medium sized sauce pan over medium-low heat.

Add water and cover for a few minutes. Remove the lid and add garlic powder and sea salt. Cover the pan and let sit for 5 to 10 minutes before serving. The Brussels sprouts should have a crunch but still be tender.

———————————————————

SEASONED STEAMED BROCCOLI

Broccoli has many nutrients that can be quickly cooked away. Steaming is a great way to prepare this wonderful vegetable. Make broccoli a fun vegetable for children by slicing it into long sticks like little trees. Children love finger foods. Add an extra treat by letting them dip the broccoli in a little vinaigrette dressing or French dressing.

Servings: 2 to 3
Prep Time: Approximately 5 minutes
Cook Time: Approximately 5 minutes
Difficulty: Easy

Ingredients:
    2 heads of fresh broccoli
    3 tbsp of Braggs Sesame Ginger Dressing
    1 tsp of ginger
    Dash of sea salt

Directions:
Using a stainless steel pot, cover the bottom of the pan with just enough water to cover and bring to a boil.

Wash the broccoli, chop it, and then add it to the boiling water. Cover and let steam for about 5 minutes or less. Then remove the lid from the pan and add Braggs ginger, dash of salt and serve. Broccoli should be slightly tender but crisp.

SPINACH SAUTÉ

Servings: 3
Prep Time: Approximately 10 minutes
Cook Time: Approximately 5 minutes
Difficulty: Easy

Ingredients:
    2 bunches of spinach (remove the roots if still attached)
    1 to 2 tsp of safflower oil
    Dash of garlic powder
    Sea salt
    Dash of white pepper

Directions:
Thoroughly wash the spinach because the leaves can contain grit. Heat a stainless steel pan on medium-high heat and add oil. Lightly sauté the spinach and add seasonings. It should be ready within a few minutes. For a change, you can add a few strips of nondairy cheese or a little Earth Balance®.

QUICK SALAD

You should eat at least one salad a day.

Servings: 2
Prep Time: Approximately 10 minutes
Difficulty: Easy

Ingredients:

½ head of romaine lettuce
1 chopped or grated large carrot
Chopped onion to taste
2 radishes or ¼ cup grated daikon radish
¼ chopped cucumbers in the summer (cucumbers cool the body)
2 tbsp Bragg® Ginger Sesame Dressing or another high quality dressing

Directions:

Using a colander, make sure you thoroughly wash the lettuce and other veggies. Add a little peroxide, fruit and veggie spray, or alkaline to tap water or use water from your water purifier. Dry the vegetables with a paper towel.

Gently tear the lettuce. Line a medium sized bowl with several sheets of paper towel to absorb the excess water from the lettuce. Add the leaves to the bowl. Place the other chopped veggies on top and lightly toss in the dressing. Enjoy!

Raw salads are full of nutrients and natural enzymes that help us to digest our food. It just makes sense that if you want to feel alive then eat live foods. Filling up on a nice size salad will help curb your appetite for heavier food. Feeding the body the right nutrients will not only help you feel better, but you won't want as much fattening food later.

QUICK DELICIOUS VEGETABLE STIR FRY

I made this one night when I was hungry and short on groceries. This dish includes great vegetables and protein. My taste buds were satisfied, and I felt full. Always keep carrots, onions and, broccoli in the fridge. Adding a few slices of firm tofu will provide extra protein.

Servings: 1 to 2
Prep Time: Approximately 10 min
Cook Time: Approximately 10 min
Difficulty: Easy

Ingredients:

5 cauliflower florets
3 spears of broccoli
1 tbsp of sliced onion
1 carrot, peeled and sliced
2 tbsp of sesame or safflower oil
Sea salt
½ teaspoon of powdered ginger
Hand-full of raw cashews
Spray of Braggs® Amino Acid *(this adds much flavor and depth to many dishes)*

Directions:

Use a stainless steel pan. Over medium-heat, add oil and allow to heat for a minute or two.

Then add onion and sauté for a couple of minutes. Add the rest of the vegetables and sauté for about five minutes. Aldd the cashews and the rest of seasonings and cook for a few extra minutes.

This recipe is a healthy serving for one person. If you want to provide more servings, you need to increase carrots, cauliflower, and broccoli. Enjoy.

CHAPTER 20
Beans & Peas

LIMA BEANS

Lima beans have lots of fiber and other vital nutrients. I enjoy the frozen organic Whole Foods Brand 365®Everday Value. The beans are tender and don't take long to prepare.

Servings: 5 to 6 (as a side item)
Prep Time: Approximately 5 minutes
Cook Time: Approximately 15 minutes
Difficulty: Easy

Ingredients:
   1 package of organic lima beans
   Sea salt
   White pepper
   1 to 2 teaspoons of Earth Balance

Directions:
In addition to the package instructions, add a teaspoon of dried parsley and use Earth Balance instead of butter or other oils. This gives the beans a butter flavor without the saturated fat.

Always remember to only use sea salt or sea salt seasoning combinations in your dishes.

BLACK-EYED PEAS

Servings: 4 to 5
Prep Time: Approximately 5 minutes
Cook Time: Approximately 45 minutes
Difficulty: Easy

Ingredients:

1 cup of dried black-eyed peas (preferably organic)
3 cups of water (adjust the water depending on how much pot liquor you desire)
1 medium onion chopped or cut in half
1 bay leaf
2 tbsp of safflower oil
1 tsp of powder or freshly grated ginger
1 inch strip of Kombu seaweed (rinse and soak for 5 to 10 minutes before adding to the pot)
1 tsp of honey
Sea salt to taste
White pepper to taste

Directions:

Soaking the peas

Rinse the peas and discard any damaged ones. You can soak the peas by placing them in a medium bowl and covering with water. Or use the quick method by adding the peas and Kombu to a medium pot filled with three cups of water. Bring to a brisk boil for about five minutes. Turn off the heat and cover the pot and let sit for an hour.

If you choose to soak the peas over night, you may want to add a little more water just so that the peas are almost floating in the pot. The peas will not swell much more after the overnight soaking.

Cooking the Peas

Turn the heat to medium-low, add onion, bay leaf and safflower oil. Simmer for about 30 minutes or until the peas are tender. Add the sea salt and pepper to taste.

Do not use as much salt because the Kombu seaweed naturally contains salt. The Kombu also adds minerals to this dish and helps to stop bloating. The seaweed taste is not noticed in this dish.

After the peas have completed cooking, add fresh or dried ginger, along with honey. Boiling kills the digestive properties of the ginger.

WHITE BEANS AND BROWN RICE

This dish is a good meat substitute.

Servings: 4 to 5
Prep Time: Approximately 10 minutes
Cook Time: Approximately 45 minutes
Difficulty: Easy

Ingredients:

    1 package of dried navy or great northern beans
    1 medium chopped yellow onion
    1 tbsp of dried parsley
    1 inch piece of Kombu (a Japanese seaweed found in health food store)
    1 teaspoon powdered ginger
    ¼ teaspoon of cumin
    2 tbsp of safflower oil
    Dash of nutmeg
    Sea salt to taste
    White pepper to taste
    ½ Bunch of washed, chopped fresh parsley

Directions:

Rinse and prepare the beans according to the package directions. Do not use chicken broth as suggested on package. By not adding the broth, this limits the sodium content.

Place the soaked Kombu Seaweed in the bottom of the pot. Pour in the beans.

I prefer to cook by the quick method. So, bring the water and beans to a boil for five minutes.

Turn off the heat and cover the beans, let it sit for approximately one hour. Add onion and oil and turn the heat to medium-low. After cooking for 45 minutes, add the reminder of the seasonings.

Check the tenderness of the beans. If they are tender, turn off the heat and add the sea salt, white pepper, and chopped fresh parsley.

Eat with a green salad and brown rice.

Brown Rice

Prepare according to package directions. Use Earth Balance or Safflower oil instead of butter. To be creative, add cayenne pepper.

CHAPTER 21
Healing Soups

RED MISO
Good for boosting the immune system and for helping the stomach. This is a good soup to serve before dinner or lunch.

Servings: At least 4
Prep Time: Approximately 15 minutes
Cook Time: Approximately 15 minutes
Difficulty: Easy

Ingredients:
- 4 to 5 cups of water
- 1 medium onion, sliced
- 1 head of broccoli, chopped
- 2 carrots, peeled and sliced
- 3 stalks of kale
- 1 tbsp of grated ginger
- 3 tbsp of red miso paste
- 2 tbsp of fresh or dried parsley
- 3 tbsp of sesame oil

Directions:
Wash all the vegetables well. Remove the large stalks from the kale. In a deep stainless steel pot, bring water to a light boil. Add sliced onion and sesame oil to the water, and let cook for a few minutes before adding the kale. Cook for another five minutes. Add broccoli and carrots turn heat on low. Do not bring to boil again.

Pour one cup of the pot's liquid into a medium glass or ceramic bowl. Add miso paste, one tablespoon at a time, by gently smashing the miso into the sides of the bowl. This will slowly dissolve the miso paste. After the paste is dissolved, add it back to the original pot. Then add the grated ginger. Steep a few minutes before serving but do not boil after the ginger is added. The ginger has many healing properties that can be destroyed if boiled.

RICH VEGETABLE SOUP

Servings: 2 to 3
Prep Time: Approximately 15 min
Cook Time: Approximately 20 min
Difficulty: Easy

Ingredients:

 3 cups organic low sodium vegetable broth
 1 cup of water
 ½ medium chopped onion
 2 medium chopped red potatoes
 1 cup of chopped or sliced fresh green cabbage
 1 tbsp dried parsley
 1 tsp dried ginger
 ½ tsp rosemary
 2 tbsp of safflower oil
 1 package of organic frozen mixed vegetables (peas, carrots, corn etc)
 1 tbsp agave sweetened organic ketchup (this is a secret that gives the soup a great taste)
 Sea salt to taste
 White pepper to taste

Directions:

Using a large stainless steel pot, pour in the broth and water, turn heat to medium.

Add onion, oil and chopped potatoes. Cover and bring to a boil, then turn the heat down to medium-low. Cook until the potatoes are just tender.

Add the frozen vegetables and chopped green cabbage. Cook for approximately 10 minutes. Add parsley, rosemary, dried ginger, and ketchup and gently stir to incorporate the seasonings. Add sea salt and white pepper to taste.

CHAPTER 22
Starch Sides

Whenever I ask people what vegetables they have eaten on that day, they always include potatoes and corn.
No, that doesn't count; these are starches. So please don't just eat these items thinking that you've had your veggies for the day.

BAKED SWEET POTATOES

Directions: Serving: One medium potato per person
Prep Time: A few minutes
Cook time: Varies depending on potato size, generally 30 to 45 minutes
Difficulty: Easy

Directions:
Preheat oven to 350 degrees F.

Wash and dry the sweet potatoes. Gently rub the potatoes with safflower oil and pierce each potato a couple of times with a fork. Bake until the potatoes are soft.

Sweet potatoes bake faster than white potatoes, so check them after 30 minutes by gently pushing a knife through the middle. When the knife easily goes through the middle of the potato, it is ready.

STOVE TOP SWEET POTATOES

Servings: 3 to 4
Prep Time: Approximately 5 minutes
Cook Time: Approximately 25 minutes
Difficulty: Easy

Ingredients:

2 large sweet potatoes
Water enough to cover the potatoes in a medium pot
2 tbsp of raw turbinado or coconut sugar
1/2 tsp of cinnamon
1 tbsp of Earth Balance®

Directions:

After you wash and peel, slice potatoes to one inch thickness.

Place the potatoes in a medium pot and bring to a boil. Turn heat on medium, and cook until you can easily put a knife through a slice easily, but not until the potatoes are mushy.

Lightly toss in the sugar and cinnamon and add the Earth Balance®.

MACARONI AND CHEESE

Suggestions for a healthier recipe

You can use your typical recipe, but substitute your typical saturated fat ingredients with a healthier selection. I usually make a quick recipe on top of the stove, unless I am making it for a family gathering. If I am, I then will use a traditional casserole dish and bake it in the oven for about 10 minutes.

My recipe uses non-dairy milk and cheese. Try to keep an open mind and give it a try. Health food stores offer a variety of non-dairy cheese and milk products. They offer cheddar, American, and other types in the non-dairy form.

Substitute Ingredients:

Almond, oat, soy or rice milk instead of diary milk
Non dairy cheese
Spelt or whole grain macaroni product (check the fiber content of the product)
Earth Balance® instead of margarine (this is a product that is non-hydrogenated)

OVEN FRIED RED POTATOES

Safflower oil is lighter than the typically used vegetable oil. This method cuts down on the frying and added fat from vegetable oil, so keep it light! If you are feeding a large family, add 1 additional tablespoon of safflower oil to three additional medium potatoes.

Servings: 3 or more
Prep Time: Approximately 5 minutes
Cook Time: Approximately 20 minutes
Difficulty: Easy

Ingredients:
    2 to 3 medium red potatoes
    2 tbsp of safflower oil
    Dash of sea salt
    Dash of white pepper

Directions:
Preheat oven to 350 degrees F.

Wash potatoes and remove any black specks from the skin while maintaining as much of the skin as possible. Dry the potatoes and slice into french fry wedges.

Place wedges in a bowl and toss with safflower oil.

Spread wedges out onto a cookie sheet, using as much of the sheet as possible.

Bake until the edges of the potatoes are lightly brown or broil on low. If you choose to broil the potatoes, you have to pay close attention because broiling cooks at a much faster rate.

Turn potatoes over once. After potatoes are lightly brown, take out of the oven and lightly season them with sea salt and white pepper.

CHAPTER 23
Delicious Hot Drinks

Hot drinks are great for the holidays or just to warm the stomach and spirit.

HOT CAROB DRINK

Try this instead of chocolate. (See the benefits of carob)

Servings: see below
Cook Time: Less than 10 min
Difficulty: Very Easy

Ingredients:
   2 tsp of powdered carob powder per 1 cup
   Almond or other organic non-dairy milk
   1 tsp of honey or agave syrup if diabetic
   Dash of cinnamon and nutmeg

Directions:
Select a small stainless steel pot over medium-low heat; pour in your choice of non-dairy milk (1 cup per serving).

Whisk in carob powder. Then add honey or agave.

Heat milk, but don't boil. Once the milk is heated through, turn off the heat and stir in the sweetener. Add cinnamon and nutmeg.

Enjoy!

HOT APPLE CIDER

Servings: One cup for each person
Cook Time: Approximately 10 minutes
Difficulty: Easy

Ingredients

One cup of apple cider
2 to 4 cinnamon sticks per each three cups
3 to 5 cloves per each three cups

Directions:

In a stainless steel pot, add cinnamon sticks and a few cloves to one each cup of cider. Steep for about 10 minutes and enjoy!

HOT GINGER TEA

Kukicha, Bancha, or green tea can be used for everyday use. There are many other herbal teas that can be used for medicinal purposes. These teas contain varying levels of caffeine, but much less than coffee. The teas mentioned have high antioxidants; and it has been suggested that they help fight off heart disease and aid in fighting cancer cells, while boosting the immune system. You can also use these teas as a gargle for sore throats. (See the benefits of ginger).

Allow to steep for 10 minutes and drink plain or with honey or agave.

CHAPTER 24

Desserts

DEB'S BANANA PUDDING – No Baking Allowed

When people taste this pudding, they can't believe this recipe doesn't use any dairy products. It is rich, tasty and light. If you are concerned, the tofu doesn't have a flavor, but it gives the pudding the creamy consistency needed for the dish. Tofu is a good form of protein and calcium and it's low in calories. You will need a blender for this dish.

Servings: 4 to 5 small bowls
Prep Time: Approximately 20 minutes
Difficulty: Easy

Ingredients:

 ½ to 1 pack of Mori NU Vanilla Pudding (purchase at health food store)
 1 or 2 bananas
 1 8 oz carton of firm tofu
 2 tsp of real vanilla extract
 Whole Foods 365® Everyday Value Brand Vanilla Wafers
 ¼ cup of organic soy milk or almond milk (add a little more milk if needed)

Directions:

Combine all ingredients in a blender. Place tofu, vanilla, and soy milk in the blender first, then add the pudding package. Blend on medium speed until all ingredients are smoothly combined. So that you don't miss any of the ingredients, make sure that you stop the blender periodically to scrape the sides of the pitcher.

Prepare a medium-size glass square dish. At the bottom of the dish, arrange the cookies in rows on the bottom and around the sides. Pour the pudding over the cookies. After you smooth the pudding over the top, add cookies to decorate the edges of the dish. If you prefer, add slices of bananas on top. To decrease the sugar content of the dish, only use 1/2 of the Mori Nu Vanilla Pudding package.

THE REAL APPLE PIE
This pie has a wonderful fragrant scent that can fill the house.

Servings: 6 to 8
Prep Time: Approximately 20 minutes
Cook Time: Approximately 1 hour
Difficulty: Easy

Ingredients:

6 to 7 medium Granny Smith apples
1 cup of Turbinado Sugar
1 ½ teaspoons of cinnamon
½ teaspoons nutmeg
1 tbsp of Earth Balance® Spread
¼ tsp of sea salt

Pie Crust:

1 cup of unbleached flour
1 ½ cups of whole wheat pastry flour
¼ to ½ cup of sesame oil (works best if refrigerated)
8 tbsp of cold water

Directions:
Preheat oven to 325 degrees F.

Peel and core apples. Slice apples approximately one inch thick and place in a large mixing bowl. Add sugar and the other seasonings to the apples, stir, and set aside.

Pie Crust: In a separate bowl, sift flour and sea salt. Gradually add oil by cutting with a fork until it looks like crumbs or small peas. Then add water and gently form the dough into a ball. Separate the balls into two smaller balls, making one ball a little larger to cover the bottom of the pie plate. Using parchment or wax paper, flour the sheets. Using a floured rolling pin, roll out the pie crust . Roll as thin as possible, turn over, and flour the new side. Roll it out again until it is large enough to cover the pie plate. Using the rolling pin, roll the pie crust over the pin and gently place over the pie plate.

Press the dough down into the bottom of the plate. Pinch the edges to make it look decorative. Prick the bottom and sides of the dough with a fork.

Pour the apples and seasonings into the pie crust and place pieces of butter over the apples. Make sure that the apples are lying as flat as possible. Repeat rolling out the dough for the top crust. After it is wide enough to cover the apples, place the top layer of dough over the apples. Pinch the top layer to the sides of the bottom layer of dough.

Using the fork, gently prick the top of the dough so that steam can escape. Bake the pie for approximately an hour. Place aluminum foil under the pie plate to catch any spills in the oven.

Peach Pie
• Use 6 to 8 peaches
• Use the same recipe as the apple pie, but substitute peaches for apples.
• Add a teaspoon of flour to the top of the peaches to keep the juice from over flowing in the oven.

CHAPTER 25

Dinner Combination Ideas

Always make sure you eat a well balanced diet with a broad spectrum of different types of foods leaning more towards a plant based diet.

DINNER A
Broiled Fish
Green Salad
Collard Greens
Red Potatoes

DINNER B
Pasta *with*
Veggie Meat Sauce Salad

DINNER C
Veggie Chili
Salad

DINNER D
Broiled or baked
Veggie Chicken
Stove-Top Boiled Sweet Potatoes
Fresh String Beans with onion

DINNER E
Sautéed Fish
Wild Rice
Butternut Squash
Green Salad

DINNER F
Veggie Burger on a Whole Grain Bun
Oven Fried Red Potatoes
Green Salad

DINNER G
Lentil Soup
Green Salad
Corn Bread

PART 3

Cooking for Children

CHAPTER 26

Feeding Baby - Food Suggestions

Please remember that babies need high quality nutrients because they are rapidly growing and changing. It is also important that they are introduced to foods according to their development. The development of their teeth coincides with the development of the digestive system. Be careful not to give hard-to-digest food to babies before they develop their teeth. Brown rice cream can be given in a bottle to the infant if you need to supplement your breast milk. I learned that it is essential to drink plenty of water and eat well when breast-feeding. This will make the milk heavy enough to satisfy the infant.

Giving an infant cereal too soon could negatively influence the development of their digestive track. A symptom of an over-taxed digestive system is a rash. Please give your infants an ounce of distilled water each day. Remember the baby has been in water for 9 months, drinking from the fluid in the mother's protective sack. Why would we not continue to make sure the baby has enough fluid? Breast milk does not fully supplement enough liquid to replace water.

The following recipe is one I used for my daughter. The brown rice has to be cooked for approximately two hours in a large stainless steel pot. The recipe below is modified from the book Vegetarian Baby by Sharon Yntema

---

BROWN RICE CREAM
Servings: Several feeds, depending on the size of bottles
Prep Time: 10-15 minutes
Cook time: Approximately 2 hours
Difficulty: Medium

Ingredients:
　　1 Cup of brown rice
　　10 cups of purified water
　　½ inch of Kombu seaweed (soaked for at least 15 minutes before adding to rice)

Brown Rice Cream (*continued*)

Directions:

Wash rice and toast lightly in a dry pan stirring constantly until it turns golden and begins to pop. Do not toast too much. Never use rice that has been scorched or darkened. Add water and Kombu. Cook for about two hours on low flame and stirring occasionally. Much of the cream should start rising to the top of the pot. The rice on the bottom should be very soft. Using a clean cheese or cotton cloth, squeeze out the cream. You want to make sure that any small pieces of hull are removed. Give to the baby in a bottle. The cream should flow similar to commercial baby formula.

INTRODUCING BABY'S FIRST FOODS

Baby's first foods should be single meals once a day after the first teeth start to break through. The baby's major food source should still be mother's milk or formula. I highly recommend getting a baby food hand grinder. You can purchase at the local health food or local grocery store, drug store, Target, or Walmart. It is easy to use and easy to clean

I caution you to never give the baby regular tap water. As mentioned earlier, start giving the infant distilled water. Invest in a filter in your kitchen. This is not only necessary for the baby but also for the health of the whole family. Toddlers and children need their water! Remember, babies are not born with a sweet tooth. Don't give fruit juice at an early age but make sure they are drinking their milk and water more than anything else.

Beginning at four months

When the baby's teeth start to show you can introduce soft foods like ripe bananas, avocados, sweet potatoes, and papayas. All foods should be finely mashed. The sweet potato can be baked or boiled until very soft. Do not add any sugar to the sweet potato. Remember that baby's palettes have not been tainted by our bad habits, so please don't start at such a young and precious age.

After five months

Slowly introduce grains like soft cooked and mashed brown rice, barley, millet, and oatmeal. Start adding butternut squash, carrots, and fresh or frozen greens beans. Always make sure you are using fresh produce and organic as much as possible. Please do not use canned foods. We should want to give our babies the best quality of food to build strong, sound bodies and minds. This is also a good time to introduce homemade apple sauce. Please see recipe on next page.

After six months you can start combining foods. Start by combining two at a time. The grains should be eaten alone initially because it may be too taxing on the digestive system to digest two types of food at one time. Also remember that babies should not be introduced to a lot of sugar. Start using some pure vanilla (only use vanilla without alcohol for your baby's foods) and cinnamon to provide variety to baby's palette. This will also teach our children that we don't have to rely on sugar and salt to spice up our foods.

At seven months of age, start introducing kale, collard greens, and broccoli. No fat back or smoked turkey please. I believe feeding our daughter greens at an early age gave her an appreciation and desire for greens. At the writing of this book, she is a freshman in college, and she has to have her greens frequently! Please see my greens recipes. Modify the recipe for the baby by taking out a small portion with some of the pot liquor (an old African American term pertaining to juice from the greens) and cook until a bit more tender and put in the baby food grinder before serving.

This is also a good time to introduce organic tofu lentils and well-cooked beans to a baby for protein and other nutrients. After nine months, you can introduce ground almonds and dates for breakfast. Dates are naturally sweet, so the baby should enjoy the taste. To soften the dates make sure they are soaked in a little water before serving. Always make sure small portions are given to the baby or toddler and that it is consistent with their ability to chew or not chew. Never leave the baby unattended while eating. It only takes a second for the baby to choke.

Older babies and toddlers enjoy finger food. Steamed broccoli can be served as a finger food. Make sure you cut the stalks and heads into little trees. They will pick-up the stalks and eat the heads. Try cutting whole grain bread into small strips and serve with apple butter. You can also add almond or cashew butter to the apple butter on whole-grain bread. This is a good snack or can be used at breakfast. This is a fast way of giving your baby good food that tastes good too.

As your child grows, make sure that you are not forcing any bad eating habits on them. Find the best options that provide your baby a healthy experience with food.

HOMEMADE APPLE SAUCE

Servings: 2 to 3
Prep Time: 5 minutes
Cook Time: Approximately 10 minutes
Difficulty: Easy

Ingredients:
   1 medium Gala, Fuji or other red apple (peel, cored and seeds removed)
   ¼ cup purified water
   pinch of sea salt
   1/2 tsp pure maple syrup (only use if apples need a little sweetener) or for variety, instead of the maple syrup, a dash of cinnamon (try this after baby is 6 months old).

Directions:
Using a small pot, add the water and adjust the heat to medium low. Add chopped apples and sea salt. Bring apples and water to a boil, and then turn the heat to low. Add the maple syrup

Simmer the apples until soft. Stir and serve!

A NOTE FOR MOTHERS

We must change our minds and realize we all need help. The western mindset tells us we can do it all, but the African woman has practiced having family and close friends assist whenever a new baby is born. My mother often shared with me her experience as a child when her mother had a newborn, her aunt stayed with the family for a month. The other children were only allowed to see their mother once a day while she was rested. My mother said my grandmother stayed in bed and her bedroom much of the month with the new baby. Her aunt cooked and helped the older children with the chores.

I believe we must renew what we knew years before modern medicine; the woman's body needs time to rest and renew after childbirth. There are so many female issues in this present age, some are caused by our lack of respect for our bodies. When did we start believing we can do it all?

New mothers, please accept help or ask for it. Do not be so proud. We all need connection and support. Rest when the baby takes a nap. Eat high quality food and make sure you drink plenty of high quality water. Remember your baby is getting their nutrients from you, so if you are lacking so is your baby.

The process of birth is a miracle that we must respect. Give yourself time to heal before you sweep and vacuum. My mother and godmother did not permit me to climb stairs for a couple of weeks after Abeni was born. If you allow your body to heal, you will have less female challenges.

We do not have to prove we are super women. Being able to birth a child is evidence enough that we are!

CHAPTER 27
Tips for Fighting Childhood Obesity

This is such a sensitive subject, but one that should not be ignored. In our love for our children, we fight to find the right approach to address their needs. My mother had many words of wisdom; one saying that comes to mind is, "This didn't just happen, it's been coming for a long time." This is a true statement when we look at the state of our children's health. We have created faster ways of eating, but not better ways of feeding our families.

The pressures of raising children when time is limited possess many challenges, but not ones that cannot be accomplished. We need to change how we think about and approach food. Akua Woodbridge, PhD in Nutrition, gave a lecture that I attended in Detroit on healthy eating. She shed light on the reason why many of us are always hungry. She says that it is because we are eating foods that lack nutrients. Our bodies keep craving those nutrients and most of the fast and processed foods we eat are not really food. Many of our children are eating artificial foods that are packed with empty calories. This, along with lack of exercise, is causing childhood obesity. If we take a few moments to rethink how we eat and organize an approach, we can change the health of our children. The sun offers a natural form of vitamin D that we all need. Our children suffer from a lack of fresh air and exercise. Natural light and fresh air assist in emotional harmony that is so useful in raising healthy children

I can bear witness to the discomfort felt by being an overweight child. We were raised on good, solid food. Most of our meals were well-balanced. Our mother made sure we had fresh vegetables every day. In fact, many of my friends would stop by the house because they knew we had a big pot of greens every week. However, there was heavy consumption of ice cream, sodas, and sometimes bread. We also ate white rice once or maybe twice a week. Luckily, I lost my weight in my pre-teen years.

Our father was the ice cream and soda culprit. He also happened to be an excellent cook, along with our mother. We were known for having good food and sometimes lots of it. Although, we were raised in a loving and nurturing home, it was hard facing the real world being overweight. I was teased many times because I couldn't run as fast or as far as my class mates. This was back in the 1960s when children had to play outside and have gym. My parents were very supportive. I think my father's power of suggestion, when he told me that before I became a teenager I would lose the weight and that he wasn't worried, really helped my concern. He was exactly correct because that's what happened. After my 12th birthday, I became sick with the flu and lost about 10 pounds. That was the beginning of a much smaller teenager. However, many of our children will not experience that type of weight loss.

Tips for Fighting Childhood Obesity (continued)

We have to create environments to begin healthier living. If we do not make changes, our children will suffer from early heart attacks, strokes and diabetes. This is a serious matter; we must pay attention. Here are suggestions on how to get started:

1. Find a physician that is knowledgeable about nutrition. Don't take for granted that your doctor is aware of proper nutrition. To this day, some medical schools don't require more than a couple of classes in nutrition. Thankfully, this trend seems to be changing, especially since the public is much more aware of other alternatives to western medicine.

2. Make sure your child participates in outside activities in safe places. Go for walks in the park, around the block or the backyard, if a park is not available. Play catch or jump rope, and make it fun. Also, do jumping jacks and sit-ups with them. Sunshine is important for better health, as long as it is not prolonged. Make sure your child is drinking plenty of water. Housework is a great way to incorporate movement and develop self-discipline. If they are at least eight years old, have them sweep, mop, vacuum, and dust.

3. Make sure you read information on how foods affect the body. Our doctors should be our partners in healthy living. Ask questions, but seek information on your own as well. Being a well-informed patient puts you in a much better position for better care. In this case, we need to know what to ask to help our children.

4. Add more fresh or frozen produce to your child's diet. Try some of the recipes and give it to them without explaining all of the details. Tell them to try the food and have an open mind. Whenever I have had other young and sometimes older children visit, I would make them try my greens or other vegetables. Their parents were always surprised that I got them to eat them. I would tell them not to grow up to be narrow-minded. This would encourage them to try something new. Also, make tasting vegetables fun. If you frown when eating certain vegetables, why would you expect the child to look happy?

5. Make sure your kids eat breakfast. If they leave the house without the proper nutrients, they will over eat all of the wrong foods. Eating fresh fruit doesn't take much extra time. By adding a piece of toast and some herbal tea, that can help get them started. I would also add almond or cashew butter to the toast for protein. In the colder months, make sure that you have oatmeal or another whole-grain cereal. Keep raw almonds, pumpkin seeds, and sunflower seeds (not salted) on hand. They can eat a hand full in the morning and have them for snacks. This is a good way of providing protein and other vital nutrients.

6. Make sure your child drinks plenty of clean filtered water. Soda should be avoided and only be consumed on rare occasions. Avoid sodas like colas because they have very high caffeine and sugar content. Read the label to see how much sugar is in juices and other beverages and limit their intake.

7. Limit red meat. This will cut your grocery bill and help the health of your child. Instead, find organic poultry sales in the health food stores whenever possible. These chickens or turkeys are usually more humanly grown, and they are generally fed much healthier diets. This means your child is not consuming unnecessary hormones and other toxins. Instead of relying heavily on meat, increase beans and whole grains in their diet. Both are good sources of protein and other nutrients. There are also good vegetarian meat choices. Read the labels and choose the products which are low in sodium, sugar, and chemicals.

8. Visit farmers and urban markets to buy fresh produce at better prices. Make sure you shop for fresh produce at least once every two weeks.

9. Be a better example for your children. Encourage them to exercise by doing fun activities with friends in the backyard or at the park. Take them for a walk a few times a week. This is a good time to talk and strengthen your bond. If you aren't exercising, make sure you start. You've heard the old saying, "It's what you do and not just what you say." Begin eating healthier for you, and then you can help your family.

10. At least twice a week, set aside quality time to eat together. Sit, relax, and enjoy your food with your loved ones. This promotes conversation and bonding. This is a good time to find out what's going on in your children's lives. It's also a good time to discuss values and goals.

11. Help to build their self-esteem and set high expectations guided with love and respect by helping them to set goals. Let them know that in order to live a successful life, they must have priorities. Their health and a healthy weight must be on that list.

12. Try making the one pot recipes such as the vegetable or chicken soups that they can eat as a meal or have as a snack. If you make the food taste good, they will enjoy eating healthier food. If they like crunchy food make sure you keep firm, crisp apples and nuts on hand. If they like creamy items give those occasional frozen desserts made with coconut milk instead of cow's milk. Try to find the brands that use agave instead of white sugar for sweetener. There is always a healthier alternative but we have to be open to changing how we think about it.

Conclusion

This book was written with the hope and goal of simplifying a healthier life style by providing information and tips that most people can adopt. A change in diet must first start in your mind. I hope that this book is presented so it is enjoyable, simple to use and informative. If you have been inspired or helped by recipes or other information, I would be most appreciated if you would let me know via FaceBook/ Debra's Healing Kitchen, App: Debra' Healthy Kitchen or www.debrapeekhaynes.com.

with Love, Debra

Measurement Reference Chart

1 tablespoon = 3 teaspoons

2 tablespoons = 1/8 cup

4 tablespoons = ¼ cup

5 tablespoons + 1 teaspoon = 1/3 cup

8 tablespoons = ½ cup

10 tablespoons + 2 teaspoons = 2/3 cup

12 tablespoons = ¾ cup

8 fluid ounces (fl oz) = 1 cup

1 pint (pt) = 2 cups

1 quart (qt) = 2 pints

4 cups = 1 quart

1 gallon (gal) = 4 quarts

16 ounces (oz) = 1 pound (lb)

8 cups = ½ gallon

8 cups = 64 fluid ounces

Pinch = Less than 1/8 teaspoon

Measurement Reference Chart (continued)

Abbreviations:

tsp = teaspoon
tbsp = tablespoon
fl = fluid
oz = ounce
pkg = package
c = cup
pt = pint
qt = quart
gal = gallon
lb = pound

Metric Equivalents for Different Types of Ingredients:

Use the following chart when converting standard cup measurements to grams (weight) or milliliters (volume)

Standard Cup	Fine Powder (ex.flour)	Grain (ex. rice)	Granular (ex. sugar)	Liquid Solids (ex. butter)	Liquid (ex. milk)
1	140g	150g	190g	200g	240ml
3/4	105g	113g	143g	150g	180ml
2/3	93g	100g	125g	133g	160ml
1/2	70g	75g	95g	100g	120ml
1/3	47g	50g	63g	67g	80ml
1/4	35g	38g	48g	50g	60ml
1/8	18g	19g	24g	25g	30ml

U.S,/Standard Metric Equivalents:

1/8 teaspoon	0.5ml
1/4 teaspoon	1 ml
1/2 teaspoon	2 ml
1 teaspoon	5 ml
1 tablespoon	15 ml
2 tablespoon	25 ml

Additional References:

Food Choices Documentary
Vitamins and Minerals for A to Z with Ethno-Consciousness, Jewel Pookrum, M.D., PhD, MFS – J.E.W.E.L Publications, Inc.
The Conscious Cook, Tal Ronnen –Melcher Media
The Macrobiotic Way, Michio Kushi - Avery

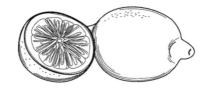

About the Author

Debra Peek-Haynes is an entrepreneur, thathas conducted seminars on health and wellness for over 25 years. Her concern regarding the wellness of others evolved from her own battle with infertility. After delivering a healthy daughter, she became passionate about sharing her story with others. It is her goal to inspire others to adopt a healthier lifestyle. Debra is well versed on the disparity of inadequate health care particularly among African Americans. Each week she can be heard live on "Let's Talk Health" a segment that provides health and wellness tips on KHVN-AM Radio. Her husband of 30 years is Dr. Frederick D. Haynes lll, Senior Pastor of Friendship West Baptist Church, a 12,000 member congregation in Dallas, Texas. She and her husband are the proud parents of their lovely daughter, Abeni Jewel.